English Grammar And Usage

Read Swiftly, Speak Fluently & Write Correctly

Prof. Shirkant Prasoon

V&S PUBLISHERS

Published by:

F-2/16, Ansari road, Daryaganj, New Delhi-110002
23240026, 23240027 • *Fax:* 011-23240028
Email: info@vspublishers.com • *Website:* www.vspublishers.com

Regional Office : Hyderabad
5-1-707/1, Brij Bhawan (Beside Central Bank of India Lane)
Bank Street, Koti, Hyderabad - 500 095
040-24737290
E-mail: vspublishershyd@gmail.com

Branch Office : Mumbai
Flat No. Ground Floor, Sonmegh Building
No. 51, Karel Wadi, Thakurdwar, Mumbai - 400 002
022-22098268
E-mail: vspublishersmum@gmail.com

Follow us on:

For any assistance sms **VSPUB** to **56161**

All books available at **www.vspublishers.com**

© Copyright: V&S PUBLISHERS
ISBN 978-93-505707-8-4
Edition 2014

The Copyright of this book, as well as all matter contained herein (including illustrations) rests with the Publishers. No person shall copy the name of the book, its title design, matter and illustrations in any form and in any language, totally or partially or in any distorted form. Anybody doing so shall face legal action and will be responsible for damages.

Printed at : Param Offseters, Okhla, New Delhi-110020

Dedication

Dedicated to all those who are eager to know, learn and use English in everyday life and prefer the direct method of Learning and Teaching. I also dedicate this book to Nishi Kant Tiwari, alias Nanhejee and to Arun Kumar Ojha, alias Barā Bābu, who made the best use of tables given in the book in their classrooms.

Publisher's Note

It has been our prime motto and a constant endeavour at **V&S Publishers** to publish books of **Value** and **Substance** from the time of its inception. With a backlist of **about 350 titles** to our credit, it's a great pleasure to inform all our esteemed readers that we have come up with this altogether exclusive series of books on **English language and its various usage** called the **EXC-EL Series – Excellence English Language Series**.

The series contains a set of books on *various usage of* Words and Phrases in English, the significance of Grammar, correct Pronunciation, etc., called *English Grammar And Usage, English Vocabulary made Easy, Improve Your Vocabulary* and *Spoken English* to enhance and enrich your vocabulary, increase your command over the language and make you more confident and fluent in your day to day conversations, written and verbal interactions, etc.

The present book, *English Grammar And Usage* is a unique one in itself **containing innumerable readymade sentences on each and every topic of Grammar** to help and enable the readers, particularly the school and college students to have an in depth understanding of the topic as well as its usage by framing sentences of their own with the given guidelines mentioned in the book.

There are **various types of Sentence Structures** available in the book in the easiest possible forms that make it all the more user-friendly, interesting and worth reading for readers of all age groups, who wish to know the language correctly and thoroughly and master it! Hope the book serves this purpose well.

Preface

As a student, I had faced many problems, so as a teacher I was in search of an easier way of learning English. Fortunately, in the late seventies of the last century, 'Structures' were introduced and made a part of the syllabus of English. In early eighties, one day, *I constructed a Table consisting of more than three thousand sentences*. I wondered: "One small page, one simple Table and three thousand sentences!" I showed that to my students, asked them to repeat the sentences. In no time, they got that pattern. I was encouraged and prepared many such Tables for them. Later on, thousands of my students wrote sentences following the Tables and learnt English well and easily. When I had a good number of Tables in my diary; the idea of a book flashed in my mind. I prepared many more tables. I took the help of Dictionaries and Reference Books on Grammar for collecting and preparing all the **Sentences** and **Verb Patterns.**

I collected and arranged all such tables and trained Shri Nishi Kant Tiwari, the Principal and Sri Arun Kumar Ojha, a teacher in Solomon Public School to teach through tables. They used to write one table in a period and the students were asked to write and orally repeat the sentences. There was one class of 'Tables' every week for each class from Std. II onwards. The students enjoyed it. They waited for the class of 'Tables' and they showed rapid progress in learning the language thoroughly.Though, at present, these teachers are not there, yet the *method of teaching English Grammar through tables* still continues in almost all the branches of that school; and thousands of students, who were taught by this process obtained scholarships in the subject in their pre-boards and boards passing out with flying colours.

In mid-nineties, I got all these tables typed and sent them to a binder. Three copies of the book were ready. The students and teachers were excited to see them as if they were printed books. However, they were not in good shape and condition, so, I got them re-typed, this time on computer.

In this book, ***Learning English through Grammar***, I have revised the above mentioned tables and also added new ones, to cover almost everything needed to complete the book in all aspects. Now, I have got an opportunity to get it published for children, teenagers, youth and elderly people (particularly the student faculty) who are always eager to learn, speak and write correct English fluently. I wish the users of this book a rapid growth in their vocabulary and a complete command over the language.

Contents

Publisher's Note 5
Preface 7
Introduction 11
How to Use the Book 13

Part-I

Chapter 1 Parts of Speech – An Introduction 17
Chapter 2 Nouns 20
Chapter 3 Pronouns 26
Chapter 4 Articles 40
Chapter 5 Adjectives 49
Chapter 6 Degrees of Comparison 55
Chapter 7 Verbs 60
Chapter 8 Agreement of the Verb with The Subject 66
Chapter 9 Gerunds 72
Chapter 10 Modal Auxiliary Verbs or Modals 76
Chapter 11 Adverbs 85
Chapter 12 Prepositions 91
Chapter 13 Conjunctions 96
Chapter 14 Interjection 99
Chapter 15 Tenses and their Uses 102
Chapter 16 Voice 120

Part-II

Chapter 1 What are Phrases and Clauses? 127
Chapter 2 The Sentence and Kinds of Sentences 131
Chapter 3 Synthesis of Sentences 136
Chapter 4 Transformation of Sentences 139
Chapter 5 Direct and Indirect Speech 146
Chapter 6 Punctuation 150
Chapter 7 Verb Patterns: Sentence Structure: Syntax 155
Chapter 8 Idioms 168
Chapter 9 Phrases, Proverbs and Expressions 175
Chapter 10 Miscellaneous Exercises 180

Introduction

The state of languages in India is steadily deteriorating. The more people talk of nourishing and improving languages, the worse is the result. Generally, most of us speak incorrect or a mixture of many languages combined together without giving the due importance to the grammar of a language. It is a fact that both Theoretical and Objective types of questions generally asked in examinations and competitions have not helped the students and aspirants much in gaining control and command over spoken and written forms of languages.

In India, Hindi is the most common language, while English is still on the driver's seat. English may not seem important for those who have to spend their whole life in local and homely atmospheres, but it's a must for all those who cherish dreams of procuring good jobs in big towns and cities or cross over the international boundaries. Every Indian should learn or try to learn English, not just to get jobs, but also to attain a respectable position in the society and to be at par with the latest developments in science and technology and the ever-changing trends of the modern society. There should not be any inhibition, prejudice or complex, while learning a language as most people have or suffer from.

First overcome all your weaknesses, if you have any, then start learning English with a free mind. You must remain conscious throughout the period you are learning the language. *Learn it with 4 Ds -- Devotion, Dedication, Determination* and *Diligence* and *5 Ps – i.e., Peace, Pleasure, Perseverance, Piety and Punctuality.* Learning this vast and rich language should give you pleasure, otherwise there is no sense in devoting your precious time and energy to it. And, when one derives pleasure out of learning, then, learning becomes entertaining like playing any sport or watching a movie, etc.

This book, **Learning English through Grammar**, will give you immense pleasure and help you learn English comfortably within a reasonable time. The **Tables**, given in the book, have been used in the classrooms with wonderful results. Students have easily and quickly learnt the structures of different types of sentences and verb patterns. Even the kids can learn the patterns by making use of the given tables and framing sentences on their own based on these patterns. This will definitely make them read and write English fluently.

This method of tables is the easiest and most convenient way of **Learning English Directly** through Tables prepared basically for those who want to READ SWIFTLY, SPEAK FLUENTLY and WRITE CORRECTLY.

One should not try the 'Translation Method' which has its own fallacies and creates problems of different nature. If the sentence in the known language is not correct or is clumsy, its translation into English will not be correct and rhythmical because every language has a syntax of its own. The syntax creates the real problem. Moreover, every language has traditional and idiosyncratic ways, and that is its beauty. The beauty of Hindi lies in the minimum number of *Prepositions* (Kāraka); and in *Gender* (Ling) that changes the pattern of the complete sentence, from nine to ninety types of *Forms of Verbs* and of course, the *exact Adjectives* on the one side and *few Adjectives* used in numerous ways, on the other.

Similarly, the beauty of English lies in apt and appropriate *Verbs, Adjectives* and *Prepositions*. It will prove a poor expression if exact Prepositions, appropriate Adjectives and commonly accepted Verbs are not used. These are the reasons that each language should be taught and learnt directly through that particular language. Most of the persons fail to speak in Sanskrit or English simply because they learn it through their mother tongue. Sanskrit would have been more popular even in other countries had it been taught in and through Sanskrit.

There is yet another reason why direct learning helps a lot. The words come easily and directly, and the sentence patterns get set in mind. Directly learning a language modulates thinking and makes one feel at home and more confident about the fact that 'these are the only ways of expressions in that language.' The teacher never says: 'There are other ways of translating that sentence.'

After letters and words, it is the sentence that makes a language. The book, *Learning English through Grammar provi*des *and teaches sentences and sentence patterns* that enable the learner to get everything well and fast. It is done through small tables that possess numerous sentences. There is no tension of syntax and words which are great hazards in translation.

Of course, on the surface, there is hardly any novelty in the Tables, but once one goes deeper, the newness and strength of these Tables come to surface. In almost every book of teaching English, particularly Grammar, there are exercises in the form of Tables to match sentences but **in Part I and Part II of this book:** *all the parts of all the columns (divisions) will match with all the other parts of the other columns (divisions). In this way, if one part from each column of a Table is taken out and joined together with the other part, it will become a correct sentence.*

Hence, the number of sentences of each table multiplies manifold as the number of parts of a sentence is multiplied with the number of the parts of other columns to bring out the exact number of sentences that can be framed from that Table.

It's really wonderful, and here lies the beauty of the book. One does not need to translate 15 or 20 similar sentences of an exercise of a book of Translation Grammar, he/ she will get numerous correct sentences from each Table: from a few dozen to a few thousands. This is the novelty of the Tables; and this makes it an excellent, authentic and perfect substitute for Translation.

I have worked hard, sincerely and diligently with utmost concentration for 18 long years to prepare these tables. It was done in the presence of students as I used to give the table, the moment it was completed, to the students of my class and asked them to write down as many sentences as they could. It was done in order to test them as well as evaluate my tables too. The number of such close examination can be imagined by multiplying the number of students writing sentences with the number of years. Incidentally, it is the 37th year. After completing most of the tables, in 16 years, I took another four years to perfect them and test them before giving them the shape of a book. *The book includes Tables and Exercises on almost each part of English Grammar.*

If one follows the instructions and speaks and writes (or speaks while writing or writes while speaking) the sentences diligently, intelligently and meticulously, one is bound to learn it within a very limited span of time. (The time will depend on the hours given every day to it, on the number of sentences written or spoken from each Table, the time taken in memorising V^1 V^2 and V^3, and on the speed of building a decent Vocabulary.) The greater the number of written or spoken sentences, the greater will be the command. The sentences and sentence patterns will start obeying, and coming faster; easily, and of course, naturally. It will give fluency to the speaker. The learner will start thinking in English, using the language as if it's his/her mother tongue.

How to Use the Book

- *Consciousness, like regularity, always pays heavy dividends. Use this book consciously and carefully.*
- *Mark and keep in mind the pattern and changes in the sentences in every Table.*
- *All the Tables are divided in to many parts. Take one (a word, a phrase or a set of words) from each part of a Table to complete a sentence. Write it or read it and proceed ahead.*
- *Don't try to match one part with another. All parts will match each other. Preferably, take in a serial order as they are written.*
- *Take one word or one set of words from each column and you will get a complete sentence. For example:*

A hawker		walking	to	the house.
A woman		coming	from	the school.
A working girl	is	going	towards	the table.
The postman				the rack.
The gardener				the board.
				(Total number of sentences: 225)

A hawker is walking to the house.
A hawker is walking from the house.
A hawker is walking towards the house.
A hawker is coming to the house.
A hawker is coming from the house.
A hawker is coming towards the house.
A hawker is going to the house.
A hawker is going from the house.
A hawker is going towards the house.
A hawker is walking to the school.
A hawker is walking from the school.
A hawker is walking towards the school.
A hawker is coming to the school.
A hawker is coming from the school.
A hawker is coming towards the school.

A hawker is going to the school.

A hawker is going from the school.

A hawker is going towards the school. ---------- And so on.

Write one complete sentence at a time. Only after completing one, write another. Don't take one part and write five or ten times, then write another part again five or ten times, then write the remaining part. This will ruin your effort. There will be no benefit by writing the sentences in parts. You have to learn the pattern, the *complete sentence structure or the Syntax.*

- *You're not a kid. No one is forcing you. It's not a task. It's not a burden. You don't have somehow show that you have written it. So, never write the sentences in parts.*
- *It's for learning the language; and you have selected the course on your own. So, write only complete sentences. Never add fragment to fragment. That way, you won't learn the pattern. Moreover, you won't learn or have command over that particular structure.*
- *Write as many sentences as you can or write all the possible sentences from each Table; but it's neither practical nor possible because in most of the Tables, the number of sentences is really very high.*
- *It's better to fix the number of sentences to be written from every Table or time-duration to be given to each Table. Take your decision after writing for a few, but once you have taken the decision; come what may; stick to that decision.*
- *It is better to give half an hour to one hour to each Table.*
- *Try your best to finish one Table in one sitting or one go. It will not give you full benefit if you write some sentences today, some the next day and some on the third day.*
- *Obviously, the Tables are divided in many parts or columns. (Take one word or one phrase or one set of words from every part or column (as given in that column) to make a meaningful sentence.*
- *The Tables are so meticulously, intelligently and correctly constructed that each part of one column will match with every other word or phrase of other parts or columns to make a meaningful sentence.*
- *If you learn the pattern during writing and speaking the sentences, then switch over to another Table; if not, then return back to that Table after a week, but not immediately. Give time to settle in.*
- *The Tables are divided in parts and sections. Without writing the sentences from the Table of one part or one section, don't move to other part or section.*
- *After finishing one section, frame at least five sentences on the pattern of that table. Then move on to another section.*
- *Learning is a slow process. Don't move fast. The faster you will move, the faster you will forget the previous one. Remember, you have to make the pattern a part of our thinking.*
- *The best way is to write as many sentences as possible in an hour from one Table.*
- *Punctuation marks are given wherever needed. Take notice of them and keep them in mind as they form a salient part of any kind of sentence.*

How to Use the Book in Schools
- The book can be given to the students of Class II onwards, but definitely from Class III. The age group 8 – 16 will learn faster by this method.
- From Class II to V, Tables can be classified and the numbers of the Tables be given to the students who must complete it. This should be made compulsory.
- If one Class per week is allotted to them, then they will get a minimum of 32 Classes in a year. This will be sufficient for the students of any class.
- They should be asked to revise the Tables done in previous class or classes to master them; and to make the sentences an integral part of their thinking.
- The students from VI onwards can use this book in various ways, such as they can read orally as well as frame and write sentences and complete as many Tables as they like in a year. Some of them may complete the book, but they should be advised to repeat it at least for three years in a row. It is apparent then, that they must own a book and can't lend it to others or depend on borrowed books.
- The teacher must guide them and be sure that the students are writing the complete sentences. The teacher should also check the tasks given to the students because if not corrected properly, students may get it all wrong.

Chapter 1

Parts of Speech – An Introduction

Words are divided into different kinds or classes, called **parts of speech**, according to their use; that is, according to the work they do in a sentence. *The parts of speech are eight in number:*

| 1. Noun | 2. Adjective | 3. Pronoun | 4. Verb |
| 5. Adverb | 6. Preposition | 7. Conjunction | 8. Interjection |

A **noun** is a word used as a name of a person, place or thing as:

    Akbar was a great *king*.   *Kolkata* is also called the '*City* of *Joy*'.

    The *rose* smells *sweet*.   The *sun* shines brightly.

His *courage* won him *honour*.

  Note: All the words in **italics** are **Nouns**.

An **adjective** is a word used to add something to the meaning of a noun; as,

  He is a *brave* boy.

  There are *twenty* boys in this class.

  Note*:* The words in **italics are **Adjectives**.

A **pronoun** is a word used instead of a noun; as,

  John is absent, because *he* is ill.

  The books are where you left *them*.

  Note: The words in **italics** are **Pronouns**.

A **verb** is a word used to say something about some person, place or thing; as,

  The girl *wrote* a letter to her cousin.

  Kolkata *is* a highly populated city.

  Iron and copper *are* useful metals.

  Note: The words in **italics** are **Verbs**.

  Is and are, also called helping verbs.

An **adverb** is a word used to add something to the meaning of a verb, an adjective or another adverb; as,

  Note: The words in **italics** are called **Adverbs**.

  He worked the sum *quickly*. (Here, it is adding to the meaning of a verb)

This flower is *very* beautiful. *(Here, it is adding to the meaning of an adjective)*

She pronounced the word *quite* correctly. *(Here, it is adding to the meaning of an adverb)*

A **preposition** is a word used with a noun or a pronoun to show how the person or thing denoted by the noun or pronoun stands in relation to something else as,

There is a cow *in* the garden.

The girl is fond *of* music.

A fair little girl sat *under* a tree.

Note: In, of and **under** are called **Prepositions**.

A **conjunction** is a word used to join words or sentences together to form a single sentence; as,

Rama *and* Hari are cousins.

Two *and* two make four.

I ran fast *but* missed the train.

Note: All the words in **italics** are **Conjunctions**.

An **interjection** is a word which expresses some sudden feeling; as,

Hurrah! We have won the game.

Alas! She is dead.

Note: The words, **Hurrah** and **Alas** are called **Interjections**.

As words are divided into different classes according to the work they do in sentences, it is clear that we cannot say to which parts of speech a word belongs to unless we see it used in a sentence.

They arrived *soon after*. (Adverb)

They arrived *after* us. (Preposition)

They arrived *after* we had left. (Conjunction)

From the above examples, *we see that the same word can be used in different parts of speech.*

Exercises

1. Name the parts of speech of each italicised word in the following sentences, giving in each case your reason for the classification:

    1. *Still* waters run deep.
    2. He *still* lives in that house.
    3. After the storm comes the *calm*.
    4. The *after effects* of the drug are bad.
    5. It weighs about a *pound*.
    6. He told us *all* about the battle.
    7. He was only a yard *off* me.
    8. Suddenly, one of the wheels came *off*.
    9. Mohammedans *fast* in the month of Ramzan.
    10. He kept the *fast* for a week.
    11. He is *on* the committee.
    12. Let us move *on*.
    13. Sit down and rest a *while*.
    14. I will watch *while* you sleep.
    15. They *while* away their evenings with books and games.

Chapter 2

Nouns

A *noun* tells us what someone or something is called. For example, name of a person (John); a job title (Doctor); a name of a thing (radio);, name of a place (Delhi); name of a quality (courage) or the name of an action (laughter). Nouns are the names we give to people, things, places, etc., in order to identify them. Many nouns are used after a determiner, e.g., a boy, this house and often combine with other words to form a noun phrase, e.g., the man next door; that big building, etc. Nouns and Noun Phrases answer the questions: 'who' or 'what'. Nouns and noun phrases may be used as:

- *The subject of a verb:*
  Our agent in Mumbai sent a message to us.
- *The direct object of a transitive verb:*
  Our agent sent an urgent message.
- *The indirect object of a verb:*
  Our agent sent a message to his manager.
- *The object of a preposition:*
  I have seen it on the paper.
- *Used in apposition:*
  Tarun, our agent sent a message.
- *Used when we speak directly to somebody:*
  "Tarun, will you come tomorrow?"

1. Go through the table given below carefully.

			a good teacher.
			a famous painter.
Jaya's	brother	is	an active politician
His	sister	was	a dull worker.
My	mother	will	a rich lawyer.
Her	father	Be	a popular doctor.
Our	uncle		a hard worker.
Their	aunt		a smooth runner.
Your	nephew		a perfect magician.

			a pop singer.
			a great artist.
			very happy.
			very tired.
			very serious.
			very angry.
			seriously ill.
			extremely happy.

Note: *You can form a maximum of about 3927 different sentences. However, write as many sentences as you can and underline the* **Nouns**.

2. **Read the table given below carefully. Make as many sentences as you can and underline the Nouns.**

	is	a bridge over the River Cauveri.
	was	a way out.
Here	was not	such a rumour.
There	will be	a meeting.
	will not be	a conference.
	has been	a great panic.
	has not been	a source of information.
	won't be	a call by the President.
	must be	a troop waiting.

Note: Here all the sentences begin with the words, 'Here' and 'There'.

Kinds of Nouns

There are five kinds of nouns: **proper, common, collective, material and abstract**.

1. A **proper noun** is the name of a particular person, place or thing:
   Akbar, Raipur, the Taj Mahal, etc.
2. A **common noun** is a name which is common to any and every person, place, or thing of the same kind:
   Student, park, statue, etc.
3. A **collective noun** denotes a number of persons or things grouped together as one complete whole:
   A crowd (a collection of people)
   A flock (a collection of sheep)
   A fleet (a collection of ships)

A distinction is made between a collective noun and a noun of multitude. A collective noun denotes a collection and hence a verb is singular; as,

The committee consists of seven members.

A noun of multitude denotes individuals of a group and hence the verb is plural although the noun is singular; as,

The committee (= the members composing the committee) quarrel among themselves.

4. A material noun denotes the matter or substance of which things are made such as: Gold, Silver, glass, cotton, steel, stone, etc.
5. An abstract noun is the name of some quality, state or action:
   Quality- kindness, goodness, wisdom.
   State- sickness, death, childhood, youth, slavery.
   Action- laughter, movement, flight, revenge.

Countable and Uncountable Nouns

If a noun is countable:
  (a) We can use 'a' or 'an' in front of it: A book, an ant.
  (b) It has a plural and can be used in a question: how many?
  (c) You can use numbers :
      One stamp, two stamps.
      Uncountable nouns

If a noun is uncountable:
  (a) We do not normally use 'a' or 'an' in front of it:
      Sugar is sweet.
  (b) It does not normally have a plural and it can be used in a question:
      How *much*?
  (c) We cannot normally use a number (one, two) in front of it.
      Give me *some* water.

A number of nouns are usually uncountable in English. A few common examples are: baggage, furniture, information, machinery, etc. eg.,

We brought *few* furniture for our house.

Give me some information on the topic.

We cannot use 'a' or a number before a mass (uncountable) noun. We cannot say a milk or two sugars. If we want to say how much milk or how much sugar, then we use a countable Noun+of (*a* bottle of milk, *two* kilos of sugar). The following are some examples of countable nouns in this pattern.

Note: *We can also use this pattern with a plural noun after 'of' e.g.,* ***a*** *packet of chips,* ***four*** *kilos of potatoes, etc.*

Collective noun + plural verb
The following collective nouns must be followed by a plural verb; these nouns do not have plural forms:

Cattle, the clergy, the military, people, the police, swine, etc.

Some people are never satisfied.

The political/the military have surrounded the building.

Noun with a plural form+ singular verb
The following nouns, though plural in form are always followed by a verb in the singular:

News: The news on T.V. is always depressing.

Games such as billiards, darts, dominoes:

Billiards is becoming more popular these days.

Names of cities, such as Athens, Naples etc.

Athens has grown rapidly in the last decade.

Two nouns joined by 'and'
Nouns that commonly go together (bread and butter, lemon and oil, fish and chips, cheese and wine, etc) are used with verbs in the singular, when we think of them as a singular unit:

Fish and chips is a popular meal.

If we think of the items as separate, we use a plural verb:

Fish and chips make a good meal.

Nouns

Exercises

1. **Form as many sentences as you can from the table below and underline the nouns. Also specify the kind of noun in each case:**

Rahul's His My Her Our Their Your	brother sister mother father uncle aunt nephew	is was will be	a good teacher. a famous painter. an active politician a dull worker. a rich lawyer. a popular doctor. a hard worker. a smooth runner. a perfect magician. a pop singer. a great artist. very happy. very tired. very serious. very happy. very angry. seriously ill. extremely happy.

Number of sentences that can be formed—3927

❑ For Example: <u>Rahul's brother</u> is a good <u>teacher</u>.
   Rahul-Proper Noun, Brother-Common Noun, Teacher—Common Noun
❑ <u>Rahul's brother</u> is very <u>happy</u>.
   Rahul-Proper Noun, Brother-Common Noun, Happy-Abstract Noun

2. **Similarly, make as many sentences as you can from the table given below and underline the nouns. Also specify the kind of noun in each case.**

   For Example: There is a <u>bridge</u> over the <u>river</u>, <u>Cauveri</u>.
   Bridge and River-Common Nouns, Cauveri-Proper Noun.

   Note: *All the sentences in the above table begin with 'There'.*

3. **Study the table given below carefully and form as many sentences as you can. Underline the nouns and also specify the type of noun in each case.**

There is	a boy	in this college.
There was	a girl	in the school.
There will be	a player	on the platform.
There is not	a doctor	in the market.
There was not	a crowd	in that street.
There will not be	a lame man	near the hall.

Note: *All the sentences in the above table begin with 'There'. Also, there is one sentence of* **Present Tense**, *one of the* **Past Tense** *and one of the* **Future Tense**, *and* **Positive** *in nature. Similarly, the last three sentences are also in Present Tense, Past Tense and Future Tense, but* **Negative** *in nature.*

Chapter 3

Pronouns

A *Pronoun* is a word that can be used in place of a noun or a noun phrase, as the word itself tells us: 'pro-noun'. For Example:
- Ravi arrived late. He had a headache.
- I wrote to my sister and told her what she should do.

Personal Pronouns

Personal pronouns refer to the speaker (first person), the person spoken to (second person), or the person, place or thing spoken about (third person). Personal pronouns must agree with nouns with the nouns in gender, number and person for which they stand:

    a. Tarun is a naughty boy.

    b. I brought a cake. It was fresh.

    c. The apples are rotten. They have to be discarded.

1. When a pronoun stands for a collective noun. It must be singular in number. If the collective noun is viewed as a single entity. If the collective noun conveys the idea of separate individuals composing the whole, then the plural number must be used:

    a. The jury has given its verdict.

    b. The jury were divided in their opinion.

2. When two singular nouns joined by 'and' refer to the same person or thing, the pronoun should be singular; as:
    - The secretary and treasurer did not do his duty.

    But when two or more singular nouns joined by 'and' and refer to different persons the pronoun is in the plural:
    - Rita and Rahul have come. They are our artists.

3. When two or more singular nouns joined by 'and' are preceded by 'each' or 'every' the pronoun must be singular:

    Each policeman and each home guard was at his post.

4. When two or more singular nouns are joined by 'or' 'either... or' 'neither... nor', the pronoun must be singular.

    Ravi or Rahul has lost his bag. Neither Ravi nor Rahul has done his work.

    But when a singular noun and a plural noun are joined by 'or' 'neither... nor' the pronoun is in the plural:
    - Neither Ali nor his friends admitted their fault.
    - Either the leader or his followers did not do their duty.

5. When a pronoun refers to more than one noun or pronoun of different persons, the pronoun agrees with the first person rather than with the second or third person, and it agrees with the second rather than with the third; as
    - He and I completed our work.
    - You and he have wasted your time.
6. With transitive verbs, the choice between the subjects form and the object form of a pronoun depends on the context and the meaning.
    You love him as much as I.
    She loves you more than me.

Reflexive and Emphasising Pronouns

Reflexive and emphasising pronouns are: Myself, yourself, himself, herself, itself, ourselves, yourselves and themselves.

   a. Used as reflexive pronouns myself, yourself etc are used as objects of a verb when the action of the verb returns to the doer. That is, in such a situation the subject and the object refer to the same person or thing: as,
   - They hurt themselves.
   - He shot himself.
   b. Used as emphasising pronouns myself, yourself etc are used to emphasise a noun or a pronoun ; as,
   - You yourself can best explain.
   - She herself can do it.

Relative Pronouns

The pronouns who, which, that, what, etc., which join two sentences and relate to nouns which have gone before are called Relative pronouns. The noun to which a relative pronoun refers is called its Antecedent.

This is the boy who gave me a pen.

In this sentence, boy is the antecedent of the Relative pronoun 'who'.

The following are the forms of the relative pronouns.

Nominative	Possessive	Objective
Who	whose	whom
Which	of which	which
That	of that	that
What	of what	what

Uses of Relative Pronouns

The relative pronoun always agrees with its Antecedent in number, gender and person.

    a. WHO is used for persons only; as:
- Blessed is he who works hard.
- God helps those who help themselves.

    b. WHICH is used for animals and for things without life; as:
He found the dog which was lost.
This is the pen which I gave you yesterday.

    c. THAT is used for persons, animals and things; as:
Uneasy lies the head that wears the crown.
He that is down need fear no fall.

    d. WHAT is used for things only. Its antecedent is always understood; as:
I say what I mean.
Attend to what he says.

Omission of the Relative Pronoun and its Antecedent

    a. The relative pronoun in the objective case is generally omitted; as:
I am the monarch of all (that) I survey.
This is the village (that) we live in.

    b. Sometimes the antecedent of a relative pronoun is omitted ; as:

    c. Whom the gods love, die young.

    d. Who laughs last laughs best.

1. **Choose the correct word from each bracket and complete the sentence.**
   - We scored as many goals as (they, them).
   - Whom can I trust, if not (she, her).
   - I am one year older than (he, him).
   - I am richer than (they, them).
   - He is as good a student as (she, her)
   - The hotel (which, what) we stayed at last summer is now closed.
   - The boy (who, whom) fell off his bicycle has hurt his leg.
   - I have not seen the boy (whose, whom) suitcase was stolen.
   - Kalidasa was a great poet (who, that) wrote interesting plays.
   - Rekha is the maid (who, whom) I have employed.

2. **Join together each of the following pairs of sentences by means of a relative pronoun:**
   - Here is the book. I told you about it.
   - Did you receive the parcel? I sent the parcel yesterday.
   - Ramesh tells lies. He deserves to be punished.
   - Here is the doctor. The doctor cured me of fever.
   - This is the man. We were saved through his courage.
   - Show me the road. The road leads to the airport.
   - The boy won the first prize. You see him sitting there.
   - They heard some news. The news astonished them.
   - She spoke to the victim. The victim's arm was in a sling.
   - he conference was a success. It was held in Pune.

1. **Make as many sentences as you can using the pronouns : It, This, That, There and Here. Underline the Pronoun in each case.**

			book.
It	is	a	bag.
This			table.
That			hat.
There			mat.
Here			torch.
			chair.
			diary.
			bottle.
			ball.
			box.
			fan.
			pencil.
			lamp.
			toy.
			bell.
			bat.
			flag.
			lock.
			key.
			kite.
			ship.
			copy.
			toffee.

Note: Take one word from each column and complete a sentence, such as:

For example: *It* is a book.
                This is a book.
                That is a book.
                There is a book.
                Here is a book.

2. **Similarly, form as many sentences as you can with the help of the pronouns: It, This, That, There given below.**

			glass.
	is not/isn't	a	gun.
It			goat.
This			cage.
That			comb.
There			cow.
			clip.
			crow.
			chain.
			bulb.
			bench.
			bed.
			bicycle.
			doll.
			drum.
			dress.
			tap.
			truck.
			train.
			tray.
			pillow.
			pot.
			plate.
			lion.
			zebra.

Note: In this case, you will get only Negative Sentences.

For example: It is not/isn't a glass, or this is not/isn't a gun.

Pronouns

3. In the next table drawn below, you have to again form as many sentences as you can with the given pronouns, it, this, that, there and here. Take one word from each column and complete a sentence. Make all the sentences you can form with the pronoun : 'it' and then begin with 'this', 'that', 'there', and so on…

Is		a	round table?	?
	it		silver pot?	
	this		black dog?	
	that		dairy farm?	
	there		rubber stamp?	
	here		smooth blade?	
			measuring tape?	
			Sunday Magazine?	
			table tray?	
			tea stall?	
			small chair?	
			red car?	
			new gun?	
			long stick?	
			golden chain.	
			leafy tree?	
			sewing machine?	
			old skirt?	
			teaspoon?	
			rose garden?	

Note: *However, in this table, all the sentences begin with 'Is', asking Questions.*

For example: *Is* **it** *a round table? Is* **this** *a silver pot? Is* **that** *a black dog?*

And so on…

4. **Make as many sentences as you can with the pronouns listed in the table given below. Select each pronoun and form as many sentences as you can. Like: It is a phone, It is a file, It is a mask, It is a register and so on…**

		is a	file	?
	It		phone	
	This		mask	
	That		register	
	There		shuttle cock	
			powerful torch	
			open basket	
			musical doll	
			beautiful calendar	
			sports shoe	
			chewing gum	
			big box	
			new bicycle	
			blue shirt	
			black dog	
			flying disc	
			night lamp	
			neck tie	
			sharp knife	
			round dish	

Note: *However, each of the sentences that are formed above ask a Question. They may not appear so, but they can be used as Questions.*

For example: *It is a phone? It is a mask? It is a file?*

And so on…

Pronouns

5. Make as many sentences as you can with the pronouns given below. However, you must pick up one pronoun and form all the sentences and then pick up the other and form all the sentences. In this way, try making as many sentences as you can. This will enhance your vocabulary and at the same time, make you thorough with pronouns.

It	is		orange.
This	was		eye.
That		an	arm.
			ant.
			iron.
			office.
			airbus.
			airship.
			airplane.
			ear.
			apple.
			axe.
			answer.
			inkpot.
			umbrella.
			asbestos sheet.
			aluminum plate.
			onion.
			onion salad.
			artistic article.

*Note: All the sentences formed above begin with **Pronouns** but have the word, 'an' instead of 'a' or 'the'. This is because they are used before words that begin with **vowel sounds**.*

6. Make as many sentences as you can with the pronouns given below.

It This That	is was	Not	An	orange. eye. arm. ant. iron. office. airbus. airship. airplane. ear. apple. axe. answer. inkpot. umbrella. asbestos sheet. aluminum plate. onion. onion salad. artistic article.

*Note: All the sentences formed above have **'an'** and are **negative sentences**.*

*Moreover, you can form both present and past tense types of sentences using **'is'** and **'was'**.*

Pronouns

7. **Form as many questions as you can with the words given below in the table.**

Is	it		Orchid	
Was	this	An	eyeball	?
	that		armchair	
			anthill	
			Iron bar	
			official flat	
			airbus term	
			airship hangar	
			airdrome	
			earring	
			apple pie	
			axe	
			answer sheet	
			inkjet printer	
			atomic umbrella	
			asbestos sheet	
			iron plate	
			easy task	
			elementary lesson	
			agricultural product	

*Note: All the sentences formed in this case will have **question marks** at their ends and will also have **'an'** in them as they are used before words beginning with **vowel sounds**.*

8. Form as many sentences as you can with the pronouns : it, this and that.

It	is	the	place.
This	was		house.
That			uniform.
			chart.
			way.
			form.
			shop.
			sweater.
			order.
			office.
			flag.
			watch.
			street.
			shirt.
			skirt.
			case.
			coat.
			ornament.
			cooler.
			cup.

Note: *All the sentences that will be formed above are both in present and past tenses and have* **'the'** *instead of* 'a' *or an* 'as' *they indicate some particular or definite object, or talk about a definite matter.*

9. Form as many sentences as you can with the words given in the table below.

It This That	is was	not	the	phone book. rule. man. pen I lost. picture he gave. photo he needs. figure I drew. toffee that I want. table of the office. bed sheet I like. call I am waiting for. camera I gave you. answer. inkpot. umbrella. asbestos sheet. aluminum plate. onion. onion salad. artistic article.

Note: All the sentences formed above will have **'the'** and **'not'**, i.e., they are basically **Negative Sentences** with 'the' in them indicating some definite objects or matter.

10. Make as many sentences as you can with the pronouns, these and those and underline the pronouns.

These Those	are were	not	authentic flags. street dogs. modern houses. pet birds. rough copies. intelligent boys. house plants. rainy coats. weather charts. race horses. steel chairs. regular beggars. green trees. old pants. new maps. Indian cows. mild animals. text books. working girls. new benches. half shirts. right keys. table fans. cheap mobiles. costly computers.

Note: Also make sure that the sentences formed from the table contain both **Positive** and **Negative** Sentences and are both in **Present** and **Past Tenses**.

For Example:

These are authentic flags.   *These were authentic flags.*
These are not authentic flags.   *These were not authentic flags.*
Those are rough copies.   *Those were rough copies.*
Those are not rough copies.   *Those were not rough copies.*

Chapter-4

Articles

The *Demonstrative Adjectives*- a,' an' and 'the'- are called articles.' A' and 'an' are called Indefinite Articles because they do not refer to any particular person or thing; as:
I saw a girl (any girl)
I ate an orange.
'The' is called the Definite article it refers to a particular person or thing; as:
I met the teacher (the particular teacher).

Indefinite Articles (A, An)

A is used before consonants, before vowels with as consonant sound and before abbreviated words with consonant sounds; as,
A man, a bird, a fruit
A unit, a university, a useful animal,
A European, a hill, a horse, a B.A., a B.ED.
An is used before vowels and before letters with a vowel sound; as,
An egg, an island, an eagle
An hour an uncle an M.A an M.L.A., an S.O.S
The indefinite article is used:
Before a singular noun which is countable
I found a pen.
I need a picture.
When a singular noun is mentioned for the first time and represents no particular person or thing:
I need a car.
I saw a child in the park
In the original sense of a/an meaning one:
A word to the wise is enough.
A stitch in time saves nine.
(In the sense of any, when an individual is meant to represent a class):
A daughter should obey her parents.
A pupil should work hard.
In exclamations before singular, countable nouns:
What a cute child! Such a long queue!
To make a common noun of a proper noun; as:
A Daniel (i.e.,) a very wise judge) came to judgment.

When we imply that a person, whose name we use with a title, in unknown to us:
A Mr. Sharma has applied for the post.
A Dr. Roy wishes to speak to you.
With names of occupations:
She'll be a dancer.
He wants to become an actor.
In expressions of speed, price and ratio:
He drives 60 kilometers an hour.
Apples cost Rs. 20, a kilo.

Definite Articles (The)
Definite article 'the' is used:
Before a noun, when a noun is known:
Anil dropped the pen.
The children were not at home.
Before nouns that are unique or are considered unique:
The sun, the stars, The equator, The Sea.
Before a noun that has become definite because it is mentioned a second time or the reader/ listener knows which one is referred to:
I bought a house in Delhi. The house is in a rural area.
Give her the pen.

Omission of the Definite Article
The definite article is not used: before the names of languages used as nouns:
I am learning to speak Italian.
He studied Urdu.
In expressions for means of travel used generally:
By air, by bus, by rail, by sea.

Use of Little, a Little, the Little and Few, a Few, the Few
Little a little and the little (adjectives) are used with uncountable nouns
Little sugar, a little sugar, the little sugar
Few, a few and the few (adjectives) are used before countable plural nouns:
Few people, a few people, the few people
There was little time for consultation.
After the famine, there was a little rice in the house.
The little rice which was available after the famine was given to the children.
The same principle is applicable to few, a few and the few eyen we refer to countable nouns:
Few towns have such splendid parks.
Our customers are poor. Only a few of them have bank accounts.
The few people who have bank accounts are illiterate.

Articles

Exercises

1. **Supply or insert** *a*, *an* or *the*, **if necessary in the following sentences and rewrite them appropriately.**
   - ❏ Bus arrived quarter of hour late.
   - ❏ Man cannot live by bread alone.
   - ❏ Physics is difficult subject.
   - ❏ They started late in afternoon.
   - ❏ At top of banyan tree, there lived eagle.
   - ❏ He likes to picturise himself as original artist.
   - ❏ April is fourth month of year.
   - ❏ Clouds over hill are lovely today.
   - ❏ May I have pleasure of your company?
   - ❏ Time makes worst of enemies friends.

1. **Form as many sentences as you can from the table below and underline the articles.**

There is	a boy	in this college.
There was	a girl	in the school.
There will be	an umbrella	on the platform.
Here is not	an apple	in the market.
Here was not	an old man	in that street.
Here will not be	a lame man	near the hall.

Note: The first three sentences are with **'There'**, and the second three sentences are with, **'Here'**. All the three tenses, **Present, Past and Future** have been indicated in the formed sentences.

2. **Go through the table carefully and form as many sentences as possible with the help of the articles, 'a' and 'the'. Also underline the articles.**

This picture		damaged	in an accident.
Her leg		shown	in the exhibition.
A new car	is	forgotten	by him.
A diner set	was	praised	outside the hall.
The fort		hit hard	in the market.
A necklace		examined	Near the Highway.

Note: All the sentences formed from the above table are both in **Present** *and* **Past Tenses** *and have both the articles,* **'a'** *and* **'the'**.

1. Complete the following sentences by filling in the blanks with 'a/an' or some:

   Example: I ought to do ____ housework.

   Answer: I ought to do some housework.

   Nitin is here for two nights, and he is looking for ____ accommodation.

   I can't fit this book into ___ bag.

   He is doing ____ research on radioactivity.

   We are just about to set off on ____ long journey.

   The people who camped in the field have left---- rubbish.

   This isn't right. Look, you've made ____ mistake.

   The scientists are doing ____ interesting experiment.

   You need ____ luck to win at this game.

   My room is quite empty. We need ___ furniture.

   I have been working on my essay. I think I've made____ progress.

   You pay extra for the taxi if you have got____ luggage.

   The second-hand shop had ____ table.

   Note: All the sentences formed from the above table will be both in Present and Past Tenses with the determiners/articles, 'a' 'an' and 'the' and also underline these words in the sentences. However, all the sentences contain 'give' and 'gave' in them. So, their formation will be different.

Determiners

We use a number of words before common nouns (or adjective common noun) which we call determiners because they affect (or 'determine') the meaning of the noun. Determiners make it clear for example which particular thing(s) we are referring to or how much of a substance we are talking about. Singular countable nouns must normally have a determiner before them.

1. **Determiners which classify or identify**
   - Indefinite article   I bought a new pen yesterday
   - Definite article   The book I am reading is expensive

Articles

- Demonstratives   I bought this/that table yesterday
- Possessives   do you like my new car?

2. **Determiners which indicate quantity**
   - Numbers   I bought two new dresses yesterday.
   - Quantifiers   I didn't buy many apples today.

There wasn't much sugar in the house.

Determiners compared with pronouns

Determiners are always followed by a noun, words such as some and this followed by a noun function as determiners. When they stand on their own they function as pronouns:

I want some water (some+noun, functioning as determiner)

    I want this   I want some

Important Determiners

Articles: a, an, the

Demonstratives: this, these, that, those

Possessives: my, our, your, his, her, its, their

Some other determiners: some, any, much, many, many a, each every, few, a few, the few, little, the little, a little either, neither, all, whole, less, fewer

1. Some, any

   Some, when used with nouns to represent things that can be counted means a few or a small number. When used with a singular noun to represent something that cannot be counted 'some' means a little or a small quantity. Some is generally used in affirmative sentences as:

   I have bought some shirts.

   Some men are born great.

   Any expresses a small number with countable nouns and a small quantity with singular uncountable nouns. Any is used in this sense in questions and negative sentences:

   Are there any files on my table?

   Is there any tea in the kettle?

2. Much, many

   Many mean a great number. Much means a large quantity. Many is used with countable nouns. Much is used with uncountable nouns; as,

   Many people went to see the film.

   I do not have many books.

3. Less, fewer

   Less denotes quantity; as,

   Please put less sugar in my coffee.

   He had less money in his pocket.

   Fewer denotes number; as,

There are fewer boys in this section than in that section.
No fewer than twenty girls were absent today.

4. All, whole
   All denotes number as well as quantity; as,
   He ate up all the sweets.
   All men are mortal.
   Whole and the whole denote quantity only; as
   We have written the whole page.
   The whole of the shop is on fire.

5. Each, every
   Each refers to one of two or more things or persons, the emphasis being on the individual whole of a group of more than two taken individually.
   Each girl will get a prize.
   Each student was given a book.

6. Either, neither
   Either means one of the two or both, as,
   There are trees, on either side of the road.
   You can go by either road.
   Neither means not either or none of the two; as,
   Neither side is winning.
   She took neither side.

7. Few, a few, the few
   'Few' means hardly any. It has a negative meaning:
   Few men reach the age of a hundred years.
   Few people are free from faults.
   A few means a small number. It has a positive meaning:
   He was asked to say a few words.
   The few means not many, but all of them.
   He lost the few friends he had.
   The few clothes the tailor had were irreparable.

8. Little, a little, the little
   Little means hardly any.
   There is little hope of the patient's recovery.
   There is little sugar left in the pot.
   A little means some, though not much.
   He has still a little money left in the bank.
   A little knowledge is a dangerous thing.
   The little means not much, but the whole of it:
   I gave to the beggar the little money I had.

Articles

1. **Fill in the blanks with some, any, each, every, either, neither:**
   - ____ side has won.
   - ____ day has its problems.
   - It rained ____ day during the holidays.
   - We have ____ money.
   - We do not have ____ rice.
   - You may have ____ of the three books.
   - ____ players did his best.
   - He may take ____ side.
   - Will you bring me ____ honey?
   - ____ man must do his duty.

2. **Fill in the blanks with many, much, all, whole, the whole:**
   - ____ students attended the class.
   - She had ____ wealth.
   - The boxer ate the ____ loaf.
   - ____ are not lovers of nature.
   - We received ____ help from our neighbours.
   - The ____ family was plunged in grief.
   - ____ men are mortal.
   - ____ a boy was present today.
   - Tagore has written ____ books.
   - I ate a ____ pineapple.

1. **Form as many sentences as you can from the table below and identify by underlining the determiners.**

I		bright eyes.
You	have /have not	steady steps.
They	(haven't)	healthy cows.
Some singers		small houses.
Five actors		new bicycles.
A few teachers		adequate sugar.
Ten workers		big gardens.
Most of the farmers		sweet voice.
Some other men		mobile phones.
A few women		mango trees.
Young nurses		many relatives.
		grown up children

Note: You can frame both Positive and Negative sentences. However, all the sentences formed will be in Present Tense.

2. **Form as many sentences as you can from the table below and identify by underlining the determiners.**

I		bright eyes.
You	had/had not	steady steps.
They	(hadn't)	healthy cows.
Some dancers		small houses.
Five actors		new bicycles.
A few teachers		adequate sugar.
Ten labourers		big gardens.
Most of the farmers		sweet voice.
Some other men		mobile phones.
A few women		mango trees.
Young nurses		many relatives.
		grown up children

Note: You can frame both Positive and Negative sentences. However, all the sentences formed will be in Present Tense.

Articles

5. Form as many sentences as you can from the table below with the determiners, 'a few' and 'many'.

There are Are there There are not	a few many	match sticks in the match boxes. books on the book shelf. flowers in my garden. flowering plants in my area. leaves on trees during winter. bags in the store.

Note: First complete all the sentences that you can make with **'a few'** and then with **'many'**, *but the maximum number of sentences which you can form will be 36. The sentences formed with* **'Are there'** *will end with* **Question Marks** *(?).*

Chapter-5

Adjectives

Adjectives literally means **'added to.'** A word which adds details to the noun (or the pronoun) or describes it is called an adjective; as,

She has a **pretty** dress.

The table is **large**.

Adjectives are used ether attributively or predicatively. We say that an adjective is used attributively, when it is placed before a noun,

    The **brave** soldier was honoured.

    It is a **bright** day.

When an adjective is used after the verb as a part of the predicate, it is said t be used predicatively:

    The soldier was **brave**.

    The day is **bright**.

A few adjectives such as old, late and heavy can take a different meaning when they are used attributively as:

    Simon peter is an **old** friend.

    My **late** grandfather was a miner.

All the words in Bold are *Adjectives* or *Describing Words*.

1. Go through the table carefully and make as many sentences as you can. Also underline all the adjectives in the following sentences.

These Those	are were		authentic flags. street dogs. modern houses. pet birds. rough copies. intelligent boys. house plants. rainy coats. weather charts. race horses. steel chairs. regular beggars. green trees. old pants. new maps. Indian cows. mild animals. text books. working girls. new benches. half shirts. right keys. table fans. cheap mobiles. costly computers.

Note: For Example: These are **authentic** flags.

These are **street** dogs.

Kinds of Adjectives

Adjectives may be divided into the following classes:

1. **Adjectives of Quality answer the question: of what kind? They show the kind of quality of a person or thing; as,**
    - He is a *clever* boy.
    - *Indian* goods are sold abroad.
    - Adjectives formed from proper nouns (e.g., *Indian* goods, *French* perfumes, *English* language, etc.) are sometimes called Proper
    - Adjectives. They are generally classed with adjectives of Quality.

2. **Adjectives of Quantity**

    Adjectives of quantity answer the question, how much? They show how much of a thing is meant; as,
    - He ate *some* bread.
    - We have had *enough* exercise.

3. **Adjectives of Number answer the question, how many, or in what order. They show how many persons or things are meant, or in what order a person or thing stands; as,**

    Take *some* ripe bananas.

    Few boys want to take risks.

4. **Demonstrative Adjectives answer the question, 'which'? They point out which person or thing is meant; as,**
    - Those girls must be rewarded.
    - This boy is brave.
    1. Interrogative Adjectives
    - Interrogative adjectives are used with nouns to ask question; as,
    - Whose shirt is this?
    - Which road leads to the town?

    2. Emphasising Adjectives
    - Emphasizing adjectives are own and very; as,
    - I saw it with my own eyes.
    - This is the very man who killed the tiger.
    3. Exclamatory Adjectives
    - What is sometimes used as an exclamatory adjective; as,
    - What an idea! What luck!
    - What a piece of work man is!

Adjectives

Adjectives Used as Nouns

Adjectives are sometimes used as nouns: as,

1. **Certain adjectives,** *preceded by the*, **can be used as nouns in the plural sense. They denote a class of persons:**
   Blessed are the meek
   The rich do not care for the poor.
2. **Some adjectives, preceded by the, denote some abstract quality:**
   The future is unknown to us.
   He admires the good.
3. **Some adjectives actually become nouns and can be used both in the singular and in the plural:**
   ❑ Junior, juniors; senior, seniors; Italian, Italians; superior, superiors; elder, elders; mortals; inferior, inferiors; Indian, Indians, etc.
4. **In certain phrases and idioms, the adjectives are used as nouns:**
   ❑ I shall see you before long.

1. **Form as many sentences as you can and underline the adjectives. Also specify the kind of adjective in each case.**

Is was	it that	not a/the	very hot day? wintery night? Sunday afternoon? month of April? a sunny day? cloudy sky? foggy weather? a dense forest? a beautiful garden? a cool evening? a delicious dish? a rough way? a mammoth gathering? the public opinion? the general rule?	?

Note: All the sentences formed from the above table end with **Question Marks** *and are* **Negative Sentences**.

2. **Form as many sentences as you can from the table given below, then identify and underline the adjectives. Also specify the kind of adjective in each case.**

There	are were		five flags. big houses. small birds. plenty of boys. tall plants. innumerable coats. black horses. uncomfortable chairs. huge trees. only blue pants. two world maps. few old cows. some religious books. a whole lot of benches. bright shirts. no keys here.

Note: All the sentences formed from the above table are **plural** *in number and are both in* **Present** *and* **Past Tenses**.

3. **Form as many sentences as you can from the table below, then underline the adjectives. Also specify the kind of adjective in each case.**

These Those	are were	not	authentic flags. street dogs. modern houses. rough copies. intelligent boys. weather charts. race horses. wild animals. working girls. cheap mobiles. costly computers.

Note: All the sentences formed from the above table are **plural** *in number and are* **negative** *in character.*

Adjectives

4. **Form as many sentences as you can from the table below, then underline the adjectives. Also specify the kind of adjective in each case.**

She He Suman A singer An actor A teacher A worker A farmer A potter	has has not	big eyes. strong legs. a new bicycle. a pot of sugar. a kitchen garden. a big house. long nose. a computer. some fruit trees.

Note: All the sentences formed will have **'Has'** *and* **'Has not'**, *i.e., they are in* **singular number** *and are of both* **Positive** *and* **Negative** *character.*

5. **Form as many sentences as you can from the table below, then underline the adjectives. Also specify the kind of adjective in each case.**

I You They Ten actors A few teachers Four workers Most of the farmers A few women Some nurses	have	bright eyes. healthy cows. small houses. new bicycles. adequate sugar. sweet voice. mango trees. many relatives. grown-up children.

Note: All the sentences formed will have **'Have'** *and* **'Have not'**, *i.e., they are in* **singular number** *and are of both* **Positive** *and* **Negative** *character.*

Chapter-6

Degrees of Comparison

An Adjective of Quality can be used in three degrees: **Positive**, **Comparative** and **Superlative**. They are called the three degrees of comparison.

Positive:
> This is a good book.
> No other book is as good as this one.
> Gold is a precious metal.
> No other metal is as precious as gold.

Comparative:
> That book is better than your book.
> Gold is more precious than copper.

Superlative:
> This book is the best of all books.
> Gold is the most precious of all metals.

Interchange of Degrees of Comparison

1. Comparative: She is taller than I
   Positive: I am not as tall as she.
2. Superlative: Gaurav is the best boy in the class.
   Comparative: Gaurav is better than any other boy in the class.
   Positive: No other boy in the class is as good as Gaurav.
3. Superlative: Mumbai is the biggest town in India.
   Comparative: Mumbai is bigger than any other town in India.

Some Important Adjectives

1. **Elder, Older. Eldest, Oldest**
   He is my elder brother
   His eldest son joined the army.
   He is the oldest man in the village.
2. **Later, Latter, Latest, Last**
   He came later than I.
   This is a later edition of the book.
   This is the latest news.
   Ravi and Harish are my friends. The former is a teacher, the latter is an artist.

I could not hear the latter part of his speech.
Ours is the last house in the street.

3. **Farther, further**
   Your house is farther from the school than mine.
   Chennai is farther from Delhi than Kolkata.

4. **Nearest, Next**
   The thief was taken to the nearest police station.
   I am leaving by the next train.

5. **Less, Fewer**
   I have less money than you.
   No fewer than sixty passengers were injured.
   No fewer than six attacks were made last night.

1. **Change the degree of comparison without changing the meaning:**
   1. Australia is the largest island in the world.
   2. A wise enemy is better than a foolish friend.
   3. Hunger is the best sauce.
   4. Very few countries are as rich as America.
   5. No other man is as strong as Atul.
   6. Shakespeare is greater than any other English poet.
   7. No other exercise is as convenient as swimming.
   8. Hyderabad is not so cool as Bangalore.
2. **Fill in the blanks with 'elder', eldest, older or oldest:**
   1. He is the ____ man in our village.
   2. She is my ____ sister.
   3. He is the ____ of the two brothers.
   4. She is ____ than Seema.
   5. Rita is the ____ girls in the school.
   6. This is the ____ temple in Goa.
   7. She is ____ than my brother.
   8. Of the two brothers Aseem is the ____.

1. **Make as many sentences as you can with the words given in the table below and underline the degrees of comparison.**

This young man		Idle	
This boy		truthful	as that.
This girl	is as	wicked	
This merchant	is not as	popular	
This river	is not so	greedy	
This manager		famous	

*Note: All the sentences formed above will be in the **Positive Degree of Comparison**.*

2. **Make as many sentences as you can with the words given in the table below and underline the degrees of comparison.**

I saw	the tallest tree.
He saw	the most beautiful city.
She saw	the highest mountain.
They visited	the oldest person.
They live near	the longest field.
We are very close to	the largest stadium.
	the biggest market.

*Note: All the sentences formed above will be in **Superlative Degree of Comparison** and should have **'the'** before the Superlative Degree.*

3. **Make as many sentences as you can with the words given in the table below and underline the degrees of comparison. Also specify the type of the degree of comparison in each case.**

This leader			of all.
This teacher		the greatest	
This young man	is	the wisest	
This boy	was	the most worthy	
This rich man	will be	more popular	
This merchant		more learned	
This river		more honest	
This leader		more diligent	

*Note: You can form as many sentences as you can but all the sentences will begin with **'This'** and end with **'of all'**.*

4. **Comparisons: Make as many comparative sentences as you can with 'is more' and 'is less'.**

This young man		idle	
This boy	is more	truthful	than that.
This girl	is less	wicked	
This rich man		popular	
This merchant		greedy	
This river		famous	
This leader		dangerous	
This manager			

*Note: All the above sentences formed will start with **'this'** and end with **'that'**, and the maximum number of sentences formed will be 147.*

5. Comparisons: Make as many comparative sentences as you can with 'is more' and 'is less'.

That young man		idle	than this.
That boy	is more	truthful	
That girl	is less	wicked	
That rich man		popular	
That merchant		greedy	
That river		famous	
That leader		dangerous	
That manager			

Note: All the above sentences formed will start with 'this' and end with 'that'. For example: That young man is more idle than this. That boy is more idle than this, That girl is more idle than this, That man is more rich than this and so on...

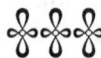

Degrees of Comparison

Chapter-7

Verbs

A **verb**, from the Latin *verbum* meaning a word (part of speech) that in syntax conveys an action (*bring, read, walk, run, learn*), an occurrence (happen, become), or a state of being (be, exist, stand). In the usual description of English, the basic form, with or without the particle to, is the infinitive. In many languages, verbs are inflected (modified in form) to encode tense, aspect, mood and voice. A verb may also agree with the person, gender, and/or number of some of its arguments, such as its subject, or object. In many languages, verbs have a present tense, to indicate that an action is being carried out; a past tense, to indicate that an action has been done; and a future tense, to indicate that an action will be done.

Examples: The words in italics in the sentences given below convey *an action or work,* such as:

1. I have been *playing* since the morning.
2. Ravi has been *staying* in Mumbai since he was five years old.
3. Raghav *does* his work neatly.
4. I have *written* his name on the blackboard.
5. My parents will be *leaving* for Canada tomorrow.

Types of Verbs

We can divide verbs into **transitive** and **intransitive verbs**.

Transitive Verbs: *These verbs involve a direct object.*

Example 1: The boy *throws* the ball.

Here 'throws' is the verb and 'ball' is the direct object.

Example 2: The man *reads* the book.

Here 'reads' is the verb and 'book' is the direct object.

Intransitive Verbs: These verbs do not involve a direct object.

Example 1: The boy *throws*.

Here the verb, 'throws' is used intransitively.

Example 2: The man reads quickly.

Here the verb, 'reads' is used intransitively.

Exercises

1. Underline the verbs in the following sentences.

1. He raised a difficult question.
2. She is good at assessing people.
3. We should de-emphasise the dangers of the situation.
4. I am returning the raincoat I borrowed.
5. The wine had been diluted.
6. I want to organize my photographs.
7. We discussed the situation.
8. May I test your bicycle?
9. You can collect the tickets at the box office.
10. Do you think they invented the whole story?

2. Underline the verbs in these sentences and specify the type in each case.

1. The mailman delivered the letter next door.
2. James calls his friends on the weekends.
3. The children played in the morning.
4. My mother usually makes tea in the morning.
5. The soldiers celebrated last week.
6. Andrea went to the beach last Sunday.
7. They stood in line for hours waiting for the doors to open.
8. He showed us his wedding album.
9. Tom forgot his homework at home.
10. The teacher just arrived.

1. **Form as many sentences as you can and identify and underline the verbs.**

I	give/gave him advice	to write a story.
We	give/gave her advice	to play outdoor games.
He		to take medicine regularly.
She		to take sweets after meal.
They		to read good books.
The teachers		to avoid overeating.
The doctor		to go to bed early.
		to walk fast.
		to munch the food.
		to draw portraits.

Note: All the above sentences are both in **Present** and **Past Tense**.

2. **Form as many sentences as you can and identify and underline the verbs.**

I		Sanskrit.
We	taught him	Hindi.
He	taught her	English.
She	gave lessons in	History.
They		Science.
The teachers		Hindi Grammar.
The doctor		Scriptures.
		Ethics.
		how to read.
		how to write.
		how to sing.

Note: All the above sentences are in **Past Tense** only.

3. Form as many sentences as you can and identify and underline the verbs. Also write the type of the verb in each case.

He	moves fast.
She	runs slow.
A man	plays well.
A boy	creates ideas.
Sohan	holds a map.
Nita	drinks juice on rare occasions.
	tells nice stories.
	works in a factory.
	carries a bag everyday.
	prefers a high stool.
	plays with mobile phones.

Note: Form all the sentences that you can with **one verb**, *then move to the* **next verb**. *In this way, make as many sentences as you can.*

4. Given below is a table from which form as many sentences as you can and underline the verbs. Also specify its type in each case.

I am	dividing the profit.
He is	learning something.
She is	walking slowly.
A boy is	forcing others.
A girl is	helping others.
The boy is	talking sweetly.
The girl is	sitting idle.
The hawker is	asking for action.
We are	paying the fare.
They are	collecting articles.
You are	throwing garbage.
The traders are	laughing loudly.
The workers are	working swiftly.

Note: All the verbs in the above sentences from the table end with **'ing'** *and are in* **Present Tense-** *denoting* **Present Continuous Tense**.

Verbs

5. **Make as many sentences as you can from the table given below and underline the verbs specifying its type in each case.**

I was	dividing the profit.
He was	learning something.
She was	walking slowly.
A boy was	forcing others.
A girl was	helping others.
The boy was	talking sweetly.
The girl was	sitting idle.
The hawker was	asking for action.
We were	paying the fare.
They were	collecting articles.
You were	throwing garbage.
The traders were	laughing loudly.

Note: All the above formed sentences are in **Past Continuous Tense**, *i.e., the work is being done in the past tense, but it's not complete and is still going on.*

6. **Form as many sentences as you can from the table below. Also underline the verb in each case.**

She	has	finished the work.
He		accepted the guilt.
The golfer		punished others.
The player		claimed the share.
The singer		visited the shrine.
The hawker		completed the task.
The shopkeeper		counted the flowers.

Note: All the above formed sentences have verbs as **'has'** *and ending with* **'ed'**.

7. **Form as many sentences as you can from the table below. Also underline the verb in each case.**

I	have/have not or haven't	finished the work.
We		accepted the guilt.
You		punished others.
They		claimed the share.
The players		visited the shrine.
The singers		completed the task.
The shopkeepers		counted the flowers.

Note: All the above formed sentences have helping verbs as **'have'** or **'have not'** (**haven't**) and the main verbs ending with **'ed'**. This is also called as the **Present Perfect Tense**.

8. **Form as many sentences as you can from the table below. Also underline the verb specifying its type in each case.**

I	had/had not or hadn't	finished the work.
We		accepted the guilt.
You		punished others.
They		claimed the share.
The players		visited the shrine.
The singers		completed the task.
The shopkeepers		counted the flowers.

Note: All the above formed sentences have verbs as **'had'** or ***had not (hadn't)*** as the helping verbs and the main verbs ending with **'ed'**. This is also called as the **Past Perfect Tense**.

Chapter-8
Agreement of the Verb with The Subject

1. *Two or more singular subjects joined by take a plural verb:*
   Rita and her sister are identical twins.
   A fool and his money are soon parted.
2. *When two subjects joined by and together express one idea, the verb is singular:*
   Time and tide waits for no man.
   Rice and dal is my favourite dish.
3. *When two singular subjects joined by and refer to the same person or thing, the verb is in the singular:*
   My friend and guide is dead.
   The poet and statesman has come.
4. *Each, everyone, either, neither, many, a must, etc., are followed by a singular verb:*
   Each of these girls tells the same story.
   Everyone was given a certificate.
   Either of the two workers is incompetent.
   Neither of these answers is correct.
   Many a boy is tempted to do mischief.
5. *When two subjects are joined by or, either.... Or, neither....nor, the verb agrees with the second subject in number and person:*
   Either he or I am to blame.
   Neither food nor water was found there.
6. *When two subjects are joined by as, well as, with, etc., the verb agrees with the first subject in number and person:*
   Manish, as well as you, is at fault.
   I, and not you, am going to act in the play.
   The king with all his sons was thrown in the dungeon.
7. *If two singular nouns joined by and are preceded by 'each' or 'every', the verb used is singular:*
   Every man and woman works for the good of this cause.
   Each and every child has completed his work.
   Every boy and girl was given a chocolate.
8. *When two subjects are joined by not only.... But, not only.... But also, the verb agrees with the second subject in number and person:*

Not only Darshan, but I am also responsible for the loss.

9. *A collective noun takes a singular verb when the class it names is considered as a unit:*
   The jury is finally complete.

10. *The following nouns though singular in form, always take a plural verb: cattle, folk, gentry majority, mankind, nobility, peasant, police, poultry, public, people, aware, etc.*
    The cattle are grazing in our field.
    Village folk wake up when the cock crows.
    The police have arrested the murderer.
    The people want justice.

11. *The following nouns which are plural in form but singular in meaning generally take a singular verb:* dynamics, economics, electronics, ethics, gallows, innings, mathematics, news, physics, statistics, summons, wages and whereabouts.
    Mathematics is an interesting subject.
    No news is good news.
    The wages of sin is death.

12. *The following nouns are plurals and have no singular form:*
    Clothes: breeches, pants, shirts socks, trousers.
    Diseases: mumps measles.
    Games: billiards, draughts.
    Tools: scissors, tongs pincers, bellows.
    Miscellaneous: alms, ashes, annals, thanks, caves, riches, tidings, proceeds, remains circumstances
    My trousers need darning at the knee.
    Mumps are common among children.
    My scissors are missing.
    Alms were given to beggars.

13. *When a plural noun denotes a quality or quantity considered as a whole, the singular verb is used:*
    Five thousand rupees is not a bad salary.

14. *When the subject is a relative pronoun, the verb must agree with the noun for which it is used:*
    Nikhil is one of the brilliant boys who have (not, has) appeared on the screen.
    Rekha is one of the prettiest actresses that have (not, has) appeared on the screen.
    This is the only one of his poems that is (not, are) worth reading.

Exercises

1. **Fill in the blanks with the correct forms of the verbs given in brackets:**
   1. The quality of pens ____ good (is/are).
   2. A white and a black cow ____ grazing in the field (is/are).
   3. Namrata, as well as her friends ____ present(is/are).
   4. Each of these minerals ____ found in India. (is/are).
   5. The chief with all his men ____ killed (was/were).
   6. The committee ____ elected its president. (has/have)
   7. He is one of the greatest leaders that ____ ever lived (has/have)
   8. If your braces ____ loose, your trousers ____ down (is/are, comes/come).
   9. The dancer and singer ____ arrived (has/have).
   10. The Arabian Nights ____ an interesting book. (is/are).

2. **Supply a verb in agreement with the subject in each of the following sentences:**
   1. What ____ the news? My glasses ____ lost and I cannot read.
   2. The voice of the singers ____ pleasant.
   3. Many an attempt ____ been made to climb Mount Everest.
   4. The shop, with all its contents, ____ insured.
   5. Which of those books ____ yours?
   6. Ten thousand rupees ____ a big sum.
   7. Neither of my uncles ____ any children.
   8. This is the only one of her poems that ____ worth reading.
   9. Either Manisha or I ____ to blame.
   10. The great poet and singer ____ dead.

1. **Make as many sentences as you can from the table below and identify and underline the verb in agreement with the subject in each case.**

			A good teacher.
			a famous painter.
Hema's	brother	is	an active politician
Rajesh's	sister	was	a dull worker.
His	mother	will be	a rich lawyer.
My	father		a popular doctor.
Her	uncle		a hard worker.
Our	aunt		a smooth runner.
Their	nephew		a perfect magician.
Your			a pop singer.
			a great artist.
			very happy.
			very tired.
			very serious.
			very angry.
			seriously ill.
			extremely happy.

*Note: All the sentences formed will be in **Present, Past** and **Future Tense**.*

2. **Form as many sentences as you can from the table below and identify and underline the verb in agreement with the subject in each case.**

There is	a boy	in this college.
There was	a girl	in the school.
There will be	a player	on the platform.
There is not	a doctor	in the market.
There was not	a crowd	in that street.
There will not be	a lame man	near the hall.

*Note: All the sentences begin with **'There'**, and are in **Present, Past** and **Future Tense**. Some are **Positive** and some are **Negative** sentences.*

3. **Form as many sentences as you can from the table below and identify by underlining the verb in agreement with the subject in each case.**

		big eyes.
She	has	strong legs.
He	has not (hasn't)	shapely arms.
Shashi		a red cow.
They		a black horse.
A singer		a new bicycle.
An actor		a pot of sugar.
A teacher		a kitchen garden.
A worker		a big house.
A farmer		a computer.
A potter		some fruit trees.

Note: All the sentences are in the **Present Tense** with **'Has'** and in **singular** number. Some are **Positive** and some are **Negative** sentences.

4. **Form as many sentences as you can from the table below and identify by underlining the verb in agreement with the subject in each case.**

		bright eyes.
I		steady steps.
You	have	healthy cows.
They		small houses.
Some singers	have not (haven't)	new bicycles.
Five actors		adequate sugar.
A few teachers		big gardens.
Ten workers		sweet voice.
Most of the farmers		mobile phones.
Some other men		mango trees.
A few women		many relatives.
Young nurses		grown up children.

Note: All the sentences have verbs in the **Present Tense** with **'Have'** and are in **plural** number. However, some are **Positive** and some are **Negative** sentences.

5. **Make as many sentences as you can from the table below and identify by underlining the verb in agreement with the subject in each case.**

She		big eyes.
He	had	strong legs.
Rekha	had not (hadn't)	shapely arms.
They		a red cow.
A singer		a black horse.
An actor		a new bicycle.
A teacher		a pot of sugar.
A worker		a kitchen garden.
A farmer		a big house.
A potter		a computer.
		some fruit trees.

Note: All the sentences have verbs in the Past Tense with **'Had'** *and* **Had not** *or* **Hadn't** *, i.e., some sentences are* **Positive** *and some are* **Negative** *Sentences.*

Chapter-9

Gerunds

A *Gerund* is a verbal noun which does the work of a verb and of a noun. A gerund being a verbal noun is used in the following ways:

As a subject of a verb, as:
Cheating should be discouraged.
Smoking is bad for health.

As the object of a verb, as:
She likes swimming.
All the boys started shouting.

As the object of a preposition, as:
They were accused of stealing.
He was prevented from visiting the spot.

As the complement of a verb, as:
What I dislike most is cheating.
My favourite pastime is bird watching.

Like a verb, it may take an object, as:
She believes in talking trash.
We are fond of singing songs.

Gerund and Infinitive

Both the gerund and the infinitive are used in the same sense. They are formed from a verb and are used as nouns; as,

Sleeping is good for health (Gerund)   To sleep is good for health. (Infinitive)
Seeing is believing (Gerund)   To see is to believe. (Infinitive)

Gerund and Present Participle

Both the Gerund and the Present Participle end in, –ing. The former is used like a *noun* and the latter is used like an *adjective*; as,

Sleeping is good for health (gerund)   A sleeping dog can be dangerous. (Present participle)
The old man was tired of walking. (Gerund).   Walking along the road, I met my friend. (Present Participle)

Exercises

1. Put the verbs in brackets into the gerund form:
1. Sunita does not enjoy (go) to the dentist.
2. I hate (borrow) money.
3. Would you mind (write) your address on the form?
4. Stop (argue) and start (think).
5. He is thinking of (make) his will.
6. Is there anything there worth (buy)?
7. It's no use (cry) over spilt milk.
8. She is looking forward to (read) your article.
9. I remember (read) a review of that film.
10. He finished (speak) and left the hall.

1. Form as many sentences as you can from the table below and identify and underline the gerunds.

Please stop	talking.
He enjoys	playing tennis.
I remember	doing it.
Please excuse	me for being so late.
Do you mind	staying a little longer?
Do you mind	my for staying a little longer?
She could not	laughing.
He keeps on	coming here.
They went on	talking.
Has it left off	raining yet.

Note: Combine each of the first part with each of the second part to frame separate sentences.

Subject + Verb	Gerund etc
He began	talking./ to talk.
He likes	swimming./ to swim.
I prefer	staying indoors./ to stay indoors.
I hate	refusing every time./ to refuse every time.
He started	packing books./ to pack his books.

Note: Form as many sentences as you can but the maximum number of sentences that you can form with the above gerunds will be: 25 + 25=50

2. Subject + Verb + Gerund

Subject + Verb + Gerund, etc.

Subject + Verb	Gerund
Please stop	talking.
He enjoys	playing tennis.
I remember	doing it.
Please excuse	me being so late.
Do you mind	staying a little longer?
Do you mind	my staying a little longer?
She could not	laughing.
He keeps on	coming here.
They went on	talking.
Has it left off	raining yet.

Note: Form as many sentences as you can with the help of the above Gerunds but the maximum number of sentences that you will get=100.

3. Subject + Verb + Gerund, etc.

Combine each of the first part with each of the second part to frame separate sentences.

Subject + Verb	Gerund etc
He began	talking./ to talk.
He likes	swimming./ to swim.
I prefer	staying indoors./ to stay indoors.
I hate	refusing every time./ to refuse every time.
He started	packing books./ to pack his books.

Note: Form as many sentences as you can with the help of the above Gerunds, etc., but the maximum number of sentences that you will get=25+25=50

4. **Combine each of the first part with each of the second part, to frame separate sentences.**

Subject + Verb	Gerund etc (Passive Infinite)
It needs	elaborating. / to be elaborated.
Your work needs	correcting. / to be corrected.
That needs	explaining. / to be explained.
He needs	refreshing. / to be refreshed.
Number of sentences	16 + 16

Note: Form as many sentences as you can with the help of the above Gerunds, etc., but the maximum number of sentences that you will get=16+16=32. Here the Gerunds, etc., are being used as **Passive Infinitives**.

Chapter-10

Modal Auxiliary Verbs or Modals

It is rude to say to a stranger, "Open the door," Normally, you would say to him: "*Will* you open the door" Or "*would* you open the door?" Or "*could* you open the door?" Verbs such as *would, will* and *could* are called *Modal Auxiliary Verbs* or *Modals.* These are often used to produce a particular effect and the modal you choose depends on several factors, such as the relationship you have with your listener, the formality or informality of the situation, and the importance of what you are saying.

Here is a list of the modals used in English:

Can	could	
May	might	
Must	ought to,	
Shall	should	
will	would	
Dare	need	need to

Dare, need to and *used to* are called **semi-modals**.

Characteristics of Modals

Modals are called defective verbs because they cannot be used in all tenses and moods.

Study the following sentences:

He might come soon.

You should learn your lessons.

I can sing that song.

She must do her work.

We notice from these sentences that

    a. A modal verb is never used alone. It must have a principal verb with as,
- Might come, should learn

    b. The modal verb used in the present tense have the same form throughout, whatever be the person and the number of the subject as,
- I can sing. You can sing. He/she can sing. They can sing.
- I may read. You may read. He/she may read. They may read.

c. The modals do not have the infinitive or participle forms. We do not say: to shall, to must, to may etc.

However, in cases where we write to will, to dare, to need, etc. the verbs will, dare and need are used as principal verbs and not as Modal Auxiliaries.

Let's consider the use of modals one by one.

1. **Shall**

    (i) In Assertive sentences, *shall,* in the first person, gives information about the future action; as,
    - I *shall* be much obliged to you.
    - We *shall* reach Delhi today.

    (ii) *Shall*, in the second and third persons, is used to denote:

    (a) A *promise*; as,
    - She *shall* have the book tomorrow
    - They *shall* have a holiday tomorrow.

    (b) A *command*; as
    - They *shall* not play there.
    - You *shall* love your neighbor as yourself.

    (c) Determination; as,
    - They *shall* work hard.
    - You *shall* do what he has told you.

    (d) A *threat*; as,
    - He *shall* be punished if he does not obey them.
    - They *shall* pay for this negligence.

    (iii) In interrogative sentences *shall*, used in the first person, indicates simple futurity, wish or opinion of the person spoken to; as,
    - *Shall* I buy this book for you?
      (Do you wish that I should buy this book for you?)
    - *Shall* we visit the museum?
      (Do you permit us to visit the museum?)

2. **Will**

    (i) In Assertive Sentences, *will* in the second and the third persons, indicates pure future; as,
    - She *will* go to Kanpur on Monday.
    - They are confident you *will* pass the examination.

(ii) In Assertive sentences, *will* indicates a customary or characteristic action, when used in the second or the third person; as,

- She *will* sit there for hours waiting for her son to come.
- Whenever he is in trouble, he *will* go to his father.

(iii) *Will,* in the second and third persons, expresses a belief or an assumption on the part of the speaker; as,

- They *will* know it.
- Mohit *will* be back now.

(iv) *Will,* in the first person is used to denote

    (a) Promise; as

        We will do better next time.

        I will teach him math.

    (b) Threat; as,

        I *will* dismiss you.

        We *will* expose her.

    (c) Willingness; as,

        Don't worry; we *will* lend you some money.

        I *will* carry your bag to office.

    (d) Determination; as,

        I *will* succeed in the venture.

        We *will* not surrender.

(v) In Interrogative sentences, *will* in the second person, denotes willingness, intention or wish of the person spoken to; as,

    Will you have a cup of coffee?

    Will you leave Mumbai on Sunday?

3. **Should**

Should is used:

(i) To denote duty or obligation; as,

    We should obey our elders.

    She should control her temper.

(ii) To denote a condition, supposition, possibility, etc; as,

    If it should rain, we shall have a holiday.

    If he should come, ask him to wait.

(iii) To indicate a concession; as,

    We will not believe it though an angel should come from heaven and say it.

(iv) When giving and asking advice; as,

You should not play with fire.

You should forgive those who hurt you.

(v) After 'lest' to express a negative purpose; as,

He worked hard lest he should fail.

(vi) To disapprove something that was done in the past; as,

They should not have laughed at her.

I should not have gone for the picnic.

(vii) In Idiomatic expression; as,

He should think so. (He is quite sure of it)

4. **Would**

Would is used:

(i) To express determination: as,

She would have her own way.

The doctor said he would visit my ailing father every day.

(ii) To express a wish; as,

I would like to see his house.

(iii) To express frequent past actions; as,

After lunch he would have a short nap.

He would sit for hours watching the stars.

(iv) To indicate refusal; as,

The wound would not heal quickly.

The engine would not start.

(v) In polite expressions; as,

Would you mind explaining this to me?

Would you please lend me some money?

(vi) To denote condition or uncertainty; as,

Had he met me I would have told him everything.

If he were clever, he would resist this offer.

5. **May**

May is used:

(i) To express permission; as,

You may use my pen for the day.

May I come in, sir?

(ii) To express a purpose; as,

   She flatters so that she may win favors.

   We eat that we may live.

(iii) To denote possibility; as,

   It may snow tonight.

   I may be elected president.

(iv) To express a wish; as,

   May you have the best of luck!

   May her soul rest in peace!

6. *Might*

   (i) Might is used to denote a possibility that is more doubtful than 'may'; as,

      She might pass.

      The patient might recover.

   (ii) Might is also used to denote extreme politeness during a discussion as: Might I have a chance to speak?

      If I might request you, couldn't you teach us history?

   (iii) Might is used to denote a gentle reproach or admonition; as,

      Well, if you were not well, you might have told me this before.

      You might tell me the truth.

7. *Can, could*

   (i) Can and could are used to express possibility, that is, some action or event is possible; as,

      Can her statement be true?

      We could succeed if we worked together.

   (ii) Can and could are used to express ability or power; as,

      I can swim

      She could dance well at the age of ten.

   (iii) Can and could are used to express permission; as,

      Can I go to see a movie?

      You can leave the office, now.

   (iv) Could sometimes do not indicate past time. It is also used to express a polite request; as,

      Could I have your book?

      Could I have a word with you?

8. *Need*
   (i) As a principal verb, need is used in the sense of 'stand in need of' or 'require'; as,
   She needs my help.
   They do not need your help.
   (ii) As an auxiliary verb, it expresses necessity or obligation and is used only in the present tense (for all persons). It is used only in interrogative and negative sentences.
   (a) In negative sentences:
   He need not seek my permission.
   We need not worry. We have been provided for.
   (b) In interrogative sentences:
   Need she do it again?
   Need I go to the hospital today?
   (c) Need as a modal auxiliary doesn't have a past form. The past is expressed with need have in questions and needn't have in negative sentences; as,
   Need they have gone on strike? (They did go on strike.)
   They needn't have bought this house.

9. *Dare*
   Dare is used:
   (i) To denote 'challenge' or 'defiance' in affirmative sentences; as,
   How dare she behave in this manner?
   He dares to call you a thief
   (ii) To denote 'venture' and courage' in negative sentences; as,
   I dare not ask him to teach me.
   She dares not tell him lies.
   (iii) To make interrogative sentences; as,
   Dare he say such a thing to me?
   Does he dare to imply that I am dishonest?

10. *Must*
    Must is used to express:
    (i) Fixed determination; as,
    I must have my money back.
    She must learn physics.
    (ii) Necessity, compulsion or strong moral obligation; as,
    We must be loyal to our country.
    I must finish the work today.

(iii) Inevitability; as,

One day man must die.

(iv) Certainty or strong likelihood; as,

She must have died by this time

Mary must have missed the train.

(v) Duty; as,

We must pay our school fees on time.

A soldier must be loyal.

(vi) Prohibition or command; as,

Students must not eat in the classroom.

11. *Ought (to)*

Ought (to) is used:

(i) To denote strong probability; as,

You ought to secure full marks in math.

(ii) To denote duty; as,

We ought to love our country.

We ought not to walk on the lawn.

12. *Used (to)*

Used (to) is used:

(i) To express a discontinued habit; as,

She used to live in this house some years ago.

There used to be some trees in this field.

(ii) To denote a repeated action, as,

When he was young he used to play football.

She used to dance before marriage.

(iii) 'Used to' also means accustomed to: as,

I am not used to hard manual labor.

They are used to a cold climate.

Exercises

1. Fill in the blanks with 'shall, will, should or would'.
   1. We ____ speak the truth.
   2. A dog _____ always remains faithful to his master.
   3. Amit said that he ____ not talk to her any more.
   4. A self-respecting man____ rather die than tell lies.
   5. As you sow, so _____ you reap.
   6. You _____ be punished if you don't do the work.
   7. The old man is walking with care lest he ____ stumble.
   8. If I were you, I ____ not do it.
   9. If today is Saturday, tomorrow _____ be Sunday.

2. Fill in the blanks with 'need, used to, ought to dare or must'.
   1. He _____ call on me today.
   2. Pupil's ____ respect their teachers.
   3. How ____ you enter my house?
   4. One _____ obey the traffic rules.
   5. A judge ___- be honest.
   6. He ____- to do this heavy work.
   7. They ___-- go out on Sundays.
   8. ____ I remind you of your promise?
   9. It ___ be done with great care.
   10. He ____ not write to his grandfather.

3. Fill in the blanks with 'must, needn't, can, could, may, might, ought to, and should'.
   1. ____ my friend live long!
   2. You ____ have been more careful.
   3. Criminals___ be punished.
   4. She ____ speak French when she was seven years old.
   5. It ____ happen, but I don't think it will.
   6. A cook ____ prepare the food with care.
   7. We ____ always obey our superiors.
   8. Visitors____ not go beyond this limit.
   9. I ____ help you if I have time.
   10. We ____ hear people talking in the hall.

Modal Auxiliary Verbs or Modals

1. **Make as many sentences as you can with the words given in the table below and identify the modals by underlining them.**

I shall	run	for an hour
We shall	play	for a prize.
They shall	go	for health.
He will	sing	for growth.
She will	stay	for a position
The teacher will	sleep	for a medal.
The tutor will	drink	in the field.
The passenger will	drive	in dress.
The player will	call	in the school.
The girls will	cry	
The clerks will		

Note: All the sentences formed above will be in **Simple Future Tense** *or* **Future Indefinite Tense**, *and you can make as many as 990 sentences.*

2. **Make as many sentences as you can with the words given in the table below and identify the modals by underlining them.**

I shall		encouraging others.
We shall	be	discouraging others.
They shall		blaming others.
He will		praising others.
She will		talking in vain.
The teacher will		delivering a lecturer.
The tutor will		carrying the bag.
The passenger will		typing a letter.
The player will		starting the computer.
The girls will		watching the match.
The clerks will		buying a ticket.

Note: All the sentences formed above will be in **Future Imperfect Tense** *or* **Future Continuous Tense**, *and you can make as many as 121 sentences.*

Chapter-11

Adverbs

The word, *Adverb* suggests the *idea of adding to the meaning of a verb*. Adverbs tell us something about the action in a sentence by modifying a verb, an adjective, an adverb, a prepositional phrase, a sentence or a conjunction: as,

Verb	: She sang well.
Adjective	: He was awfully hungry.
Other Adverb	: We will come very soon.
Prepositional Phrase	: You are entirely in the wrong.
Complete Sentence	: Fortunately, I won the first prize.
Conjunction	: He comes here only when my father is present.

The following sentences show how adverbs affect the meaning of a sentence. Compare:

Harry has left.   Harry has just left.
I have finished work.   I have nearly finished work.

Kinds of Adverbs

There are three kinds of adverbs: simple, interrogative, and relative.

Simple Adverbs

Simple adverbs modify words. They can be divided into the following groups:

1. Adverbs of time (which show when): now, then, before, soon, tomorrow, already etc:
   The president is now in his office.
   I have spoken to the principal already.

2. Adverbs of place (which show where): here, there, everywhere, in, out, etc:
   He looked for me everywhere.
   He had come here.

3. Adverbs of manner (which show how or in what manner): well, badly, thus, so, etc.
   Slowly and sadly we laid him down.

4. Adverbs of frequency (which show how often): once, twice sometimes, seldom, etc.
   I have often made mistakes. He has already met me twice.

5. Adverbs of degree or quantity (which show how much or to what extent or in what degree) : very, much, almost, wholly, quite, extent, rather, etc:
   The water is very cold. The weather is very pleasant.
   He is altogether mistaken.

Adverbs

6. Adverbs of reason (therefore, likewise, etc.):
   She is hence absent from school.
   He was, therefore, put in detention.
7. Adverbs of affirmation or negation (yes, certainly, surely, no, never, etc):
   I shall certainly attend the meeting.　　　He will never come.

Interrogative Adverbs

These adverbs are used in asking questions; as,

1.	Time	: when will you come again?
2.	Place	: where are you going?
3.	Manner	: how do you intend helping me?
4.	Number or frequency	: how many people were present?
5.	Degree, extent or quantity	: how deep is the well?
6.	Reason	: why did you do this?

Relative Adverbs

Relative adverbs modify some word in a clause; they also connect the clause in which they occur with the rest of the sentence. The antecedent noun to which they relate may be either omitted or expressed.

a. The antecedent expressed : as,
   - This is the school where I studied.
   - I do not know the time when it rained.
b. The antecedent omitted; as,
   - This is where (the place in which) we met earlier.
   - I did not know when (the time by which) he had come.

Uses of Some Adverbs

1. **Too, Very,**
   - The adverb 'too' means excess of some kind or more than enough. It should not be used in place of very or much; as,
   - This news is too good to be true.
   - We shall be too late for the show.
   - 'Very' merely means much:
   - It is very hot today.　　　He is very kind.
2. **Much, Very,**
   - 'Much' is used before past participles. 'Very' before present participles
   - I was much disturbed by his behavior.
   - His behavior is very annoying even now.

- ❏ 'Much' is used with adjectives and adverbs in the comparative degree. 'Very' is used in the positive degree:
- ❏ I feel much better today.   He walked very slowly.

3. **Before, ago, since**
   - ❏ 'Before' as an adverb means formerly; as,
   - ❏ He reached here an hour before.   He has been to Shimla before.
   - ❏ 'Ago' denotes a period of time from the present dating backwards. 'Since' recons from a point of time in the past up to the present:
   - ❏ His father died three years ago.
   - ❏ He has not met me before.
   - ❏ I have not seen him since last Christmas.

4. **Fairly, Rather**
   - ❏ Both mean moderately. 'Fairly' is mainly used with favourable adjectives and adverbs while 'rather' is used with unfavourable adjectives and adverbs.
   - ❏ She is fairly rich, but her aunt is rather poor.
   - ❏ I did fairly well in the examination, but my friend did rather badly.

Exercises

1. Fill in the blanks with the suitable words:
- He spoke loud ____ to be heard. (much, enough).
- It is ____ late, but not ____ late to catch the train. (too, very)
- She waited for us ____ impatiently. (very, much)
- Fruit is ____ cheap today, but is ____ dear for me to buy any. (too, very)
- This magazine is ____ heavy, but that one is ____ light. (fairly, rather)
- This news is ____ good to be true (very, too)
- It is ____ hot to go outside. (very, much)
- Our school closed a fortnight ____ (since, ago)
- She has been absent from school ____ last Monday. (since, ago)
- The patient is ____- better today. (too, much)

2. Insert the words in the brackets in suitable places:
- We lost the match. (nearly)
- He makes a mistake. (rarely)
- He did well in the examination. (fairly)
- The pupils have completed the class work. (almost)
- I am late for my lectures. (often)
- Does he make mistakes? (generally)
- I was able to hear what they said. (hardly)
- He has travelled by train. (never)
- We deceive ourselves. (sometimes)
- I know her well. (quite)

1. **Form as many sentences as you can from the table given below and underline the adverbs. Also specify its kind in each case.**

He	does/does not(doesn't)	move fast.
She		run slowly.
It		play well.
A man		drinks juice rarely.
A boy		tell interesting stories daily.
The man		work hard in a factory.
The boy		carry a bag every day.
Sohan		play with mobile phones usually.
Neeta		

Note: Each of the sentences formed from the above table have **helping verbs, 'does'** *or* **does not (doesn't)** *followed by the main verb and an adverb in each case. However, all the sentences will be in* **Present Tense.**

2. **Form as many sentences as you can from the table given below and underline the adverbs. Also specify its kind in each case.**

He	did/did not	move fast.
She	(didn't)	run slowly.
It		play well.
A man		drinks juice rarely.
A boy		tell interesting stories daily.
The man		work hard in a factory.
The boy		carry a bag every day.
Sohan		play with mobile phones smartly.
Neeta		

Note: Each of the sentences formed from the above table will have **helping verbs, 'did'** *or* **did not (didn't)** *followed by the main verb and an adverb in each case. However, all the sentences formed will be in* **Past Tense.**

3. **Form as many sentences as you can from the table given below and underline the adverbs. Also specify its kind in each case.**

He	is/are	singing melodiously
She		writing letters continuously.
We		calling someone loudly.

Adverbs

They		going for a walk regularly.
A teacher		coming towards the temple quickly.
The manager		teaching some people occasionally.
A devotee		cleaning the table regularly.
		arranging papers neatly.

Note: Each of the sentences formed from the above table will have a **helping verb is/are**, as the case may be followed by the main verb and then the adverb. However, all the sentences will be in Present Continuous Tense, i.e., expressing the work is not complete, but is going on.

4. **Form as many sentences as you can from the table given below and underline the adverbs. Also specify its kind in each case.**

He	is/are	singing melodiously
She		writing letters continuously.
We		calling someone loudly.
They		going for a walk regularly.
A teacher		coming towards the temple quickly.
The manager		teaching some people occasionally.
A devotee		cleaning the table regularly.
		arranging papers neatly.

Note: Each of the sentences formed from the above table will have a **helping verb was/were**, as the case may be followed by the main verb and then the adverb. However, all the sentences will be in **Past Continuous Tense**, i.e., indicating that the work was not complete, but was going on.

Chapter-12

Prepositions

A *Preposition* is a word usually placed before a noun or pronoun to show its relation to 'some other word in a sentence; as,

There is a pen on the book.
She is fond of music.
Jane jumped into the river.

Uses of Prepositions

AT, IN, ON

We see you at 10 o' clock.
They began their journey at sunset.
In the next few days, In the summer holidays, In July, in the 19th century.
Make sure you are at the station in time for the train.
The 7.30 train started on time.
On arriving, on hearing…..

AT, IN AND ON: IN RESPECT OF PLACE

Someone is knocking at the door.
The car was waiting at the gate.
He lives in Moga in Punjab.
He works in Kolkata in India.
He lives at Pipri in Goa.
Look at the picture on the wall.
Spread the carpet on the floor.
Delhi is on the Yamuna.
My shop is right on the main road.

ON, UPON

She sat on a sofa.
The tiger pounced upon the deer.

IN, INTO

The fish is in the water.
Mohan jumped into the swimming pool.

IN, WITHIN

I will return in a month. (at the close of)
I will return within a month. (in less than)

IN, AFTER
They shall finish the construction in a week.
He reached Mumbai after two days.
FOR, SINCE, AGO
I stayed in Delhi for a week.
Please wait for five minutes.
I have lived here since 1975.
I haven't met her since September.
I joined the school nine years ago.
We came to your house two months ago.
BETWEEN, AMONG
Divide the bananas between the two children.
A dispute arose between the landlord and the tenant.
The four sisters quarreled among themselves.
There is said to be an understanding among thieves.
BESIDE, BESIDES
They sat beside him.
Besides being fined, they were imprisoned.
TILL/UNTIL, BY
He sat in the shop till/until closing time.
I'll be working in the office till/until next June
I get up by 6 o'clock.
Please return my book by Monday.
BY, WITH
She stood by her father.
He sat by himself.
She eats with me, talks with me and walks with me.
With all her faults, I love her.
BEFORE, FOR
He shall be there before 8 o'clock.
We shall not be there before 4 o' clock.
ABOVE, OVER
The aeroplane flew above the clouds.
High above us an eagle was hovering.
The bridge over the river is long.
The aeroplane flew over the town.

Exercises

1. **Choose a suitable preposition from the options given in each bracket.**
   - The children sat (on/upon) the ground.
   - One should live (in/within) one's means.
   - We must trust (in/on) our close friends.
   - The train is (after/behind) time.
   - Three thieves quarreled (between/among) themselves.
   - He arrived (by/with) all his belongings.
   - She was (in/at) Kolkata last night.
   - She has been ill (since/for) last night.
   - We will return (in/on an hour.
   - We returned from the picnic (after/since) three days.

1. **Subject + Verb + Direct Object + Preposition + Prepositional Object**

Subject + Verb		Preposition	
I gave	the money	to	my friend.
They told	the news	to	everybody they met.
We showed	the pictures	to	our teachers.
I do not lend	my books	to	anybody.
He offered	once	to	me.
I owe	30 rupees	to	my tailor.
Throw	that box	to	me.
Bring	that book	to	me.

Note: Combine the first part with the second part and use the preposition,' to' to form eight different types of sentences.

2. Subject + Verb + Direct Object + Preposition + Prepositional Object

Subject + Verb	Direct Object	Preposition	Prepositional object
He bought	a necklace	for	the bride.
He gifted	a gold watch	to	his wife.
Please give	some	for	me.
They left	a message	for	the commander.
She made	a new dress	for	herself.
Have you left	any	for	your sister.
Please get	two tickets	for	me.
They selected	a bride	for	their son.

Note: Form as many sentences as you can using appropriate prepositions from the above table and the maximum number of sentences that you can get will be = 8

3. Subject + Verb + Direct Object + Preposition + Prepositional Object

Subject + Verb	Direct Object	Preposition	Prepositional Object
Thank	You	for	your kind help.
Ask	him	for	a few more.
Compare	this	with	that flag.
They punished	him	for	being very late.
Congratulate	him	on	his grand success.
Do not throw	the stone	at	the poor donkey.
What prevented	you	from	joining the post?
Add	this	to	what you have.
I explained	my difficulty	to	the manager.
Protect	us	from	the terrorists.

Note: Form as many sentences as you can using appropriate prepositions from the above table and the maximum number of sentences that you can get will be =10

4. Form as many sentences as you can and identify by underlining the prepositions.

		is calling me.
	under the tree,	is playing a game.
The girl,	at the window,	is holding a book.
The boy,	in the classroom,	is blowing a whistle.
The teacher,	on the road,	is writing a letter.
The man,		is eating a fruit.
The woman,		is driving a car.
		is asking for help.

Note: You can make as many sentences as you can, but all the sentences formed will be in Present Continuous Tense or Present Imperfect Tense indicating that the work is under process and not complete.

5. Form as many sentences as you can and identify by underlining the prepositions.

		is not calling me.
The girl,	above the tree,	is not playing a game.
The boy,	behind the window,	is not holding a book.
The teacher,	near the classroom,	is not blowing a whistle.
The man,	across the road,	is not writing a letter.
The woman,		is not eating a fruit.
		is not driving a car.
		is not asking for help.

Note: You can make as many sentences as you can, but all the sentences formed will be Negative in nature and in **Present Continuous** or **Present Imperfect Tense**.

6. Form as many sentences that you can form and underline the prepositions.

			book		
There is		a	pen	at	the table.
There was			pencil	on	the box.
There will be			chalk	near	the bag.
			lamp	by	my copy.
			knife	away from	that radio.
			slate	close to	the computer.
			ring	across	his diary.
			key	under	

Note: The maximum number of sentences that you can form will be 405. Underline all the prepositions.

✤✤✤

Prepositions

Chapter-13

Conjunctions

A *Conjunction* is a word which joins together *two words* or *two clauses*; as, I eat bread and butter.

Two and two *makes* four.

Correlative Conjunctions

Conjunctions which are used in pairs are called Correlative Conjunctions; as,

Either.... Or: Either he is a fool or he is a rogue.

Neither....nor : Neither a borrower nor a lender be.

Both... and : He was both praised and rewarded.

Not only .... But also: Not only is he foolish, but also obstinate.

Whether... or: I do not care whether you eat or not.

Co-ordinating Conjunctions

These join together words, *phrases* or *clauses* of *equal rank*. They are of *four kinds*:

Cumulative conjunctions:

Pay your taxes **and** live in peace.

He is **both** a teacher **and** a preacher.

Alternative Conjunctions

These express an alternative or a choice between two statements.

She must weep **or** she will die.

I have **neither** a pen **nor** a pencil

Subordinating Conjunctions

Subordinating conjunctions may be classified according to their meanings, as follows:

TIME: The train arrived **after** the signal had been lowered.

The man had died **before** the doctor arrived.

Cause and Reason: I will give up my claim **since** you insist on it.

Let us go to bed **as** it is midnight.

Concession or Contrast: Although he is poor, he is honest.

You cannot deceive him, **however** you may try.

Exercises

1. Fill in the blanks with appropriate conjunctions:
- She was ___ill___ she could not study.
- Strike ____ the iron is hot.
- ____ she is poor, ___ she is honest.
- ____ he tells the truth, he will be spared.
- I brought it ____ I needed it.
- Many strange things have happened ___ they came here.
- Take heed ____ you fall.
- Please write ____ she dictates.
- Make hay ___ the sun shines.
- Rita is pretty ____ not proud.

2. Join each pair of sentences into one by using a suitable conjunction: One has been done for you.
- *Example: Rita has no time to answer your call as she is late.*
- We will go for an outing. We will do so if the weather is fine.
- We had better get ready now. We may not have time to reach the airport.
- Mr. Harry has been sick. He has been so since coming back from Japan.
- Do not start the rehearsal yet. The chairman has not arrived.
- The debating teams were very happy. Both were declared joint-champions.
- The players gave their best. They still did not win the match.
- The boys were unhappy with their results. The girls were also unhappy with theirs.
- Let us be more serious in our revision. We may not perform as well as we want.

1. **Form as many sentences as you can and identify by underlining the conjunctions.**

Is Was	the dog the cat the horse the bag the car the scooter mobile phone	white or black big or small red or gray mine or yours cheap or costly ugly or attractive simple or majestic	?

Note: All the sentences formed will end in Question Marks and the total number of sentences formed will be equal to 98.

2. **Identify and underline the conjunctions in the sentences given below.**
   - ❏ The thief ran away when he saw the guard.
   - ❏ Aunt will get angry if you do not come soon.
   - ❏ He won the race even though he participated unwillingly.
   - ❏ The sky turned cloudy and it began to rain.
   - ❏ The boy became sad when the girl started crying.
   - ❏ The girl looks innocent even though she is very clever.
   - ❏ She continued to study though she had finished her course.
   - ❏ The old man did not walk because he was very weak.
   - ❏ We will attend the party even if you do not return back in time.
   - ❏ I like to go to the countryside because it is free from pollution.

Chapter-14

Interjection

Examine the following sentences:
Hello! What are you doing here?
Alas! He is dead.
Hurrah! We have won the game.
Ah! Have they gone?
Oh! I got such a fright.
Hush! Don't make a noise.
Hello! Alas! Hurrah! Ah! Etc. They are called Interjections.
They are used to express some sudden feeling or emotion. It will be noticed that they are not grammatically related to the other words in a sentence.
An interjection is a word which expresses some sudden feeling or emotion.
Interjection may express-
Joy; as Hurrah! Huzza!
Grief; as, alas!
Surprise; as, ha! What!
Approval; as, bravo!
Certain groups of words are also used to express some sudden feeling or emotion; as,
Ah me! For shame! Well done! Good gracious!

The following is a list of some commonly used interjections in sentences:
- *Ah* - *Ah*, what a delicious meal!
- *Aha* - *Aha*, now I see what you mean!
- *Alas* - I love football but, *alas*, I have no talent as a player.
- *Eh* - *Eh*? Say it again - I wasn't listening.
- *Er* - "Is he handsome?" "*Er*, well - he's got a nice friendly sort of face though he's not exactly handsome."
- *Hello* - *Hello*, Paul. I haven't seen you for ages.
- *Hey* - *Hey*! What are you doing with my car?

- *Hi* - *Hi*, there!
- *Hmm* - "He says he's doing it for our benefit." "*Hmm*, I'm still not convinced."
- *Oh* - Is that for me? *Oh*, you're so kind!
- *Well* - *Well*, what shall we do now?

The following are the main interjections, arranged according to the emotions which they are generally intended to indicate:

Of joy; eigh! hey! io!

Of sorrow; oh! ah! hoo! alas! alack! lackaday! welladay! or welaway!

Of wonder; heigh! ha! strange! indeed!

Of wishing, earnestness, or vocative address; (often with a noun or pronoun in the nominative absolute;) O!

Of praise; well-done! good! bravo!

Of surprise with disapproval; whew! hoity-toity! hoida! zounds! what!

Of pain or fear; oh! ooh! ah! eh! O dear!

Of contempt; fudge! pugh! poh! pshaw! pish! tush! tut! humph!

Of aversion; foh! faugh! fie! fy! foy!

Of expulsion; out! off! shoo! whew! begone! avaunt! aroynt!

Of calling aloud; ho! soho! what-ho! hollo! holla! hallo! halloo! hoy! ahoy!

Of exultation; ah! aha! huzza! hey! heyday! hurrah!

Of laughter; ha, ha, ha; he, he, he; te-hee, te-hee.

Of salutation; welcome! hail! all-hail!

Of calling to attention; ho! lo! la! law! look! see! behold! hark!

Of calling to silence; hush! hist! whist! 'st! aw! mum!

Of dread or horror; oh! ha! hah! what!

Of languor or weariness; heigh-ho! heigh-ho-hum!

Of stopping; hold! soft! avast! whoh!

Of parting; farewell! adieu! good-by! good-day!

Of knowing or detecting; oho! ahah! ay-ay!

Of interrogating; eh? ha? hey?

Exercises

1. **Fill in the blanks with the correct Interjections in the sentences given below.**
   - ☐ _____, that feels good!
   - ☐ _____, she's dead now!
   - ☐ _____! Does it hurt ?
   - ☐ _____! What do you think of that ?
   - ☐ _____! Didn't you know Lima is the capital of Peru.
   - ☐ _____ John, How are you today ?
   - ☐ _____, I'm not so sure.
   - ☐ _____! 85 divided by 5 is17.
   - ☐ _____, Shall we go ?
   - ☐ _____! That hurts !

2. **Identify and underline the interjections in the sentences listed below.**
   - ☐ Hey! You left me behind.
   - ☐ Ouch! That soup is hot.
   - ☐ Oops! The plate broke
   - ☐ Well, I guess Ill go.
   - ☐ Hurray! We won the game.
   - ☐ Wow! John hit the ball far.
   - ☐ Hurry! I saw something scary in the cave.
   - ☐ Alas! I cannot go with you.
   - ☐ Shh! I heard something.
   - ☐ Ah, I see what you mean.

3. **Identify and underline the interjections in the sentences listed below.**
   - ☐ Hush! Don't disturb the class.
   - ☐ Alas! My friend has met with an accident.
   - ☐ Hurrah! They have won the match.
   - ☐ Bravo! We are going to Goa next week.
   - ☐ Ah! He is dead.
   - ☐ May he survive this crisis!
   - ☐ What a nice day!
   - ☐ How stupid of you to behave like this!
   - ☐ What a fool you are!
   - ☐ Oh! I'm having a terrible pain in stomach.

Chapter-15

Tenses and their Uses

Simple Present Tense
Simple present tense is used in expression of the immediate present
She wants to speak at once.
It is very cold.
To indicate the present period:
My father works in an office.
Our school has a big hall.
To express a situation that is permanent:
This train runs from Delhi to Mumbai.
Our office faces east.
To express general truths:
A chemical reaction takes place in the fuel cell.
The soul is immortal.
Two and four makes six.
To express regular or habitual actions:
I get up early and eat my breakfast.
I practise speaking English every day.
To express a future action:
What do we do next month?
The college reopens next Monday.
In time clauses:
When you come to Mumbai, pay us a visit.
Wait there until I come back.
In conditional clauses:
Unless you walk fast, you will be late.
If you a determined, you will succeed.
In factual writing:
Pour three cups of water and bring it to boil. Put the water in the kettle and put four teaspoons of tea leaves. After three minutes strain the tea, add milk and sugar.
In dramatic narratives:

In the film, Amit plays the central character.
The audience waits anxiously for the function to start.
In reports:
I hear you are moving.
I have never seen ice-skating, but they tell me it is a fascinating sport.

Present Continuous Tense
For something continuous is used:
For something happening at the time of speaking
 We are having a meeting. Come and join in.
What is he doing? He is looking out of the window.
To emphasise the present moment:
I am working as a teacher.
She is spending the summer in Ooty.
Planned future action:
We are going to have a debate next Saturday.
I am meeting you at the railway station tomorrow.
To indicate progressive change:
My handwriting is improving.
The situation is changing but the atmosphere is disturbed.
To denote frequent actions:
You are always looking for faults.
She is always talking to him on the telephone.
In habitual actions:
Do you know if she is still playing golf these days?
He is seeing a lot of Hindi films these days.

Present Perfect Tense
To refer to past situations that continues up to the present:
Adverbial phrases like now, before, up to the present, etc, are used with the present perfect in order to refer to the past in with the present time.
All my working life I have waited for a better future.
I have always felt that films should be entertaining.
To express a past action, the result of which still continues:
She has been ill since last Friday.
I have cared for him for seven years.
To express what happened in the past without stating a specific time:
I have read the novel, but I do not remember the details.

They have raised five lakh rupees for an auditorium

To express an action that has just been completed:

The sun has set.

We have just finished our tea.

For repeated or habitual actions:

I have often wondered why she is so generous.

He has practised the game regularly and he is sure to win.

In news broadcasts:

The government has decided to pass the bill. The decision was taken at the cabinet meeting held at 11 p.m., yesterday in the Prime Minister's office.

Use of 'Since' and 'For'

'Since' and 'for' are often used with the present perfect.

I have been here since 8 o' clock.

For is used with the present perfect tense to indicate a period of time extending into the present as,

I have been here for two hours.

Present Perfect Continuous Tense

Linking the past with the present:

I have been working in the office for ten years.

Repeated actions:

I have been asking him to help me. He refused to help.

I have asked him five times to help me. He did not help.

Drawing conclusions:

Nina eyes are red. It is obvious, she ahs been crying.

Amit has a heavy cold; he has been studying late at night.

Past Perfect Tense

Reference to the earlier past:

I met my friend in 1995. I had already met his father five years earlier.

The whole complex was in chaos. The police had demolished all the floors of the building.

To distinguish between two actions in the past

The patient had died when the doctor arrived.

She had lost her job as the manager and was working as a waitress.

In conditional clauses; as,

If I had known you were ill, I would have come to see you

Had I known the doctor was around, I should have discussed my problem with him.

Past Perfect Continuous
Time and duration

The president came back from Tokyo where he had been meeting other world leaders.

The doctor was very tired because he had been working alone.

Drawing conclusion

Amit looked tired. He had been working late at night.

Seema was fresh because she had been resting the whole day.

Repeated actions

The teacher was angry because Ravi had not been doing his work for a whole week.

Joe was annoyed. John had been phoning him every day.

Simple Future Tense
To predict what we think will happen; as,

The festival will last for a week.

One day people will travel to mars.

To indicate an offer or a promise; as,

I shall post that letter for you.

I will give you a gift, if you pass.

To indicate an instant decision (at the moment of speaking); as,

It is very hot. I will put on the fan.

It is my birthday. We will have a party.

After verbs and verb phrases like be sure, think, expect, suppose, hope, believe, etc; as,

I hope he will come tomorrow.

I'm sure it will be all right.

I expect we will win the match.

Future Continuous Tense
The future continuous tense is used to indicate an action over a period of future time. It means that we will be in the middle of an action; as,

This time next week we will be driving through Nepal.

When he leaves the building, the police will be waiting for him.

Future Perfect and Future Perfect Continuous Tenses

If you are referring to something that has not happened yet, but will happen before a particular time in the future, you can use the future perfect tense' as,

Perhaps by the time we get back home, he will already have started.

When you come back tomorrow you will have heard from your sister.

I will have retired by the year, 2005.

Different Charts of Tenses

1. Chart of Tense (Active and Passive Voice)

	the dog	white or black	
Is	the cat	big or small	?
Was	the horse	red or gray	
	the bag	mine or yours	
	the car	cheap or costly	
	the scooter	ugly or attractive	
	mobile phone	simple or majestic	

Note: Read, understand and keep the chart in mind always fresh. It covers about 60 per cent of English.

2. Present Indefinite Tense

Person	Number	Active Voice	Passive Voice
1st Person	Singular	I teach him.	He is taught by me.
	Plural	We teach him.	He is taught by us.
2nd Person	Singular	You teach him.	He is taught by you.
	Plural		
3rd Person	Singular	He teaches us.	We are taught by him.
	Plural	They teach us.	We are taught by them

3. Present Imperfect Tense

Person	Number	Active Voice	Passive Voice
1st Person	Singular	I am teaching him.	He is being taught by me.
	Plural	We are teaching him.	He is being taught by us.
2nd Person	Singular	You are teaching him.	He is being taught by you.
	Plural		
3rd Person	Singular	He is teaching us.	We are being taught by him.
	Plural	They are teaching us.	We are being taught by them

4. Present Perfect Tense

Person	Number	Active Voice	Passive Voice
1st Person	Singular	I have taught him.	He has been taught by me.
	Plural	We have taught him.	He has been taught by us.
2nd Person	Singular	You have taught him.	He has been taught by you.
	Plural		
3rd Person	Singular	He has taught us.	We have been taught by him.
	Plural	They have taught us.	We have been taught by them

Person	Number	Active Voice	Passive Voice
1st Person	Singular	I taught him.	He was taught by me.
	Plural	We taught him.	He was taught by us.
2nd Person	Singular	You taught him.	He was taught by you.
	Plural		
3rd Person	Singular	He taught us.	We were taught by him.
	Plural	They taught us.	We were taught by them

5. Past Imperfect Tense

Person	Number	Active Voice	Passive Voice
1st Person	Singular	I was teaching him.	He was being taught by me.
	Plural	We were teaching him.	He was being taught by us.

2nd Person	Singular	You were teaching him.	He was being taught by you.
	Plural		
3rd Person	Singular	He was teaching us.	We were being taught by him.
	Plural	They were teaching us.	We were being taught by them

6. Past Perfect Tense

Person	Number	Active Voice	Passive Voice
1st Person	Singular	I had taught him.	He had been taught by me.
	Plural	We had taught him.	He had been taught by us.
2nd Person	Singular	You had taught him.	He had been taught by you.
	Plural		
3rd Person	Singular	He had taught us.	We had been taught by him.
	Plural	They had taught us.	We had been taught by them

7. Future Indefinite Tense

Person	Number	Active Voice	Passive Voice
1st Person	Singular	I shall teach him.	He shall be taught by me.
	Plural	We shall teach him.	He shall be taught by us.
2nd Person	Singular	You shall teach him.	He shall be taught by you.
	Plural		
3rd Person	Singular	He will teach us.	We shall be taught by him.
	Plural	They will teach us.	We shall be taught by them

8. Future Perfect Tense

Person	Number	Active Voice	Passive Voice
1st Person	Singular	I shall have taught him.	He will have been taught by me.
	Plural	We shall have taught him.	He will have been taught by us.
2nd Person	Singular	You will have taught him.	He will have been taught by you.
	Plural		
3rd Person	Singular	He will have taught us.	We shall have been taught by him.
	Plural	They will have taught us.	We shall have been taught by them

Exercises

1. **Fill in the blanks using the simple present or the present continuous tense of the words given in brackets:**
   - Where_____ you_____ now?" "I ___ to the theatre."(go)
   - Mr. Gupta ____ (teach) us English every day. He is absent: so Mr. Kumar ____ (take) our class just now.
   - The sun ___ (rises) in the east.
   - She generally ____ a red skirt but today she ____ a green one. (wear)
   - I ____ (drink) at least six glasses of water every morning.

2. **Use the past continuous tense in the following sentences:**
   - It _____ heavily all night. (rain)
   - ____ Football yesterday? (they play)
   - I _____, so I missed what he said. (not listen)
   - I ____ whether you could lend me your car. (wonder)
   - He ____ all weekend. (garden)
   - ____ when he left? (you still work)
   - ____ when she came to you? (you read)
   - I lived in Patna, when you _____ in Delhi? (live)
   - When he was young, he _____ football. (always play)

3. **Fill in the blanks with suitable forms of verbs given in brackets.**
   - The school bus ____ at school now. It ____ there since mid-day. (wait)
   - Amit always ___ (come) to school on time.
   - She normally ____ very well but today she _____ very badly. (play)
   - The sun ___ (shine) brightly when he got up this morning.
   - I always ____ my raincoat in case it rains. I _____ my raincoat because it is likely to rain. (carry)
   - He realized that he ____ (take) the wrong road.
   - The telephone bell ___ (ring). It sometimes ____ fifty times a day. (ring).
   - Vandana said that she ____ (see) that movie before.
   - My brother ____ to the court every day. He ____ there now.(drive)
   - The old man ____ (fall) as he (cross) the street.

1. **Form as many sentences as you can and identify the Tense of the Verb in each case.**

He	moves fast.
She/ It	runs slow.
A man	plays well.
A woman	creates ideas.
A boy	holds a map.
A girl	drinks juice on rare occasions.
Sohan	tells nice stories.
Nita	works in a factory.
	carries a bag everyday.
	prefers a high stool.
	plays with mobile phones.

Note: You can form as many sentences as you can but the **Noun/Pronoun** *in the* **first person** *is in* **singular number** *in all the sentences.*

2. **Form as many sentences as you can and identify the Tense of the Verb in each case.**

I	work hard.
We	lead a tough life.
They	show great skill.
Workers	perform well.
Officers	help the society.
Players	live for others.
Writers	sense the danger in time.
Students	take safety measures.
Farmers	come in time.
Drivers	sit for hours.

Note: Except for the first sentence, in all the other sentences, the **Noun/Pronoun** *in the* **first person** *is* **plural** *in number.*

Tenses and their Uses

3. **Form as many sentences as you can and identify the Tense of the Verb in each case.**

I am	dividing the profit.
He is	learning something.
She is	walking slowly.
A boy is	forcing others.
A girl is	helping others.
The hawker is	talking sweetly.
We are	sitting idle.
They are	asking for action.
Traders are	paying the fare.
Workers are	collecting articles.
Peons are	throwing garbage.

Note: Make as many sentences as you can and the maximum number of sentences you will get is 121.

4. **Form as many sentences as you can and identify the Tense of the Verb in each case.**

She	has	finished the work.
He		accomplished all.
The golfer		accepted the guilt.
The player		punished others.
The singer		claimed the share.
The hawker		visited the shrine.
The shopkeeper		completed the task.
		created some space.
		controlled the crowd.
		counted the flowers.
		shown the way.

*Note: Make as many sentences as you can but the **Noun/Pronoun in the first person** in all the sentences will be in **singular number**.*

5. **Form as many sentences as you can and identify the Tense of the Verb in each case.**

I	have	finished the work.
We		accomplished all.
Boys		accepted the guilt.
Girls		punished others.
His pupils		claimed the share.
My sons		grown up strong.
The salesmen		visited the shrine.
The representatives		completed the task.
The workers		controlled the crowd.
		counted the flowers.
		shown the way.

Note: *Make as many sentences as you can but the* **Noun/Pronoun** *in the* **first person** *in all the sentences will be in* **plural number**.

6. **Form as many sentences as you can and identify the Tense of the Verb in each case.**

He	has been	worrying since the last meal.
She		trying very hard for square meals.
It		looking into water.
A porter		working since morning.
A heron		visiting places.
A hermit		searching something in the soil.
A farmer		living on the least.
I	have been	facing dangers.
We		fighting for survival.
They		wasting time.
Birds		moving aimlessly.
Animals		doing nothing.
Insects		turning again and again.
Farmers		waiting for long.
Larks		Eating slowly.

Note: *The maximum number of sentences that you can make will be 105+120=225.*

7. Present Indefinite Interrogative

Do	I	work hard?
	we	lead a tough life?
	they	show great skill?
	workers	perform well?
	officers	help the society?
	players	live for others?
	writers	sense the danger in time?
	students	take safety measures?
	farmers	come in time?
	drivers	sit for hours?

Note: Number of sentences that you will get will be 100.

1. Add **'not'** after the subject to change them into **Interrogative Negative**.

2. Work with the following table to construct sentences into **Negative**; and to change the above sentences into **Negative sentences**.

8. Present Indefinite (Negative)

I		work hard.
We		lead a tough life.
They	do not	show great skill.
Workers	don't	perform well.
Officers		help the society.
Players		live for others.
Writers		sense the danger in time.
Students		take safety measures.
Farmers		come in time.
Drivers		sit for hours.

Note: The maximum number of sentences that can be formed will be 200.

9. Simple Past or Past Indefinite

I	carried the load for a mile.
We	threw the baskets in the ditch.
He	placed the articles on the tables.
She	swept the vehicle.
They	polished the seats.
The cyclists	loaded the packets.

The drivers	crossed the city.
The traders	slowed the vehicle.
The farmers	sold the bags.
The venders	shifted the position.
	Opened the door.
	allowed only one person to sit.
	bought a healthy sheep.
	collected flowers from the backyard.

Note: You can form as many as 140 sentences, but the **Noun/Pronoun** in the **first person** will keep changing—some in **Singular Number** and the others in **Plural Number**.

10. Form as many sentences as you can and identify and underline the Tense of Verb in each case.

			some honey.
He	gave	her	some money.
She	sold	him	a few eggs.
Krishna	sent	me	one dozen mangoes.
Sheela			a nice puppy.
A hawker			a toy rabbit.
A vendor			

Note: You can form as many sentences as you can, but the **Noun/Pronoun** in the first person will be in **Singular Number**.

11. Past Imperfect or Past Continuous Tense

He	Was	singing hymns.
She		writing letters.
A worker		calling someone.
The manager		going for a walk.
A devotee		coming towards the temple.
		playing with children.
		sitting in the field.
		teaching some people.
		cleaning the table.
		arranging papers.

Note: Form as many sentences as you can but the **Noun/Pronoun** in the first person will be in **Singular Number** and the maximum number of sentences that can be formed will be 50.

Tenses and their Uses

12. Past Imperfect or Past Continuous Tense

He	Was	singing hymns.
She		writing letters.
A worker		calling someone.
The manager		going for a walk.
A devotee		coming towards the temple.
		playing with children.
		sitting in the field.
		teaching some people.
		cleaning the table.
		arranging papers.

Note: Use **was** *for the* **Noun/Pronoun** *in* **Singular Number** *and* **were** *for* **Plural Numbers** – *such as We, Children and They.*

13. Past Imperfect or Past Continuous Tense – Form as many sentences as you can but the nouns in the first person will be plural in number.

We	were	singing hymns.
The clerks		writing letters.
The priests		calling someone.
The reporters		going for a walk.
The women		coming towards the temple.
The children.		playing with children.
		sitting in the field.
		teaching some people.
		cleaning the table.
		arranging papers.

Note: *You can make a maximum of 60 sentences. Since the* **Noun/Pronoun** *in the* **first person** *are in* **Plural number***, the verb used will be 'were'.*

14. Form as many sentences as you can and identify by underlining the Tense in each case.

She	had	finished the work.
He		accomplished all.
The golfer		accepted the guilt.
The player		fined the helpers.
The singer		punished others.
The hawker		claimed the share.

I		grown up strong.
We		visited the shrine.
Boys		completed the task.
Girls		created some space.
His pupils		controlled the crowd.
My sons		counted the flowers.
The salesmen		shown the way.
The workers		

Note: The number of sentences that you can form will be equal to 208.

15. Past Perfect Continuous Tense

I	had been	crying for the payment.
We		trying to get it done.
She		staying here for long.
They		dancing on the road.
He		begging for mercy.
The beggar		throwing stones recklessly.
The pensioner		getting closer.
The helper		seeking help.
The helpless		tearing papers.
A commoner		

Note: You can form a maximum of about 90 sentences from the above table.

16. Future Indefinite Tense

I shall	run	for an hour
We shall	play	for a prize.
They shall	go	for health.
He will	sing	for growth.
She will	stay	for a position
The teacher will	sleep	for a medal.
The tutor will	drink	in the field.
The passenger will	drive	in dress.
The player will	call	in the school.
The girls will	cry	
The clerks will		

Note: You can form as many sentences as you can, but the maximum number of sentences that you can get will be 990.

Tenses and their Uses

17. Future Imperfect or Future Continuous Tense

I shall		encouraging others.
We shall	be	discouraging others.
They shall		blaming others.
He will		praising others.
She will		talking in vain.
The teacher will		delivering a lecturer.
The tutor will		carrying the bag.
The passenger will		typing a letter.
The player will		starting the computer.
The girls will		watching the match.
The clerks will		buying a ticket.

Note: You can form as many sentences as you can, but the maximum number of sentences that you can get will be 121.

18. Future Perfect Tense

I	will have/shall	finished the work.
We		accomplished all.
Boys		accepted the guilt.
Girls		fined the helpers.
His pupils		punished others.
My sons		claimed the share.
The salesmen		grown up strong.
The representatives		visited the shrine.
The workers		completed the task.
She		created some space.
He		controlled the crowd.
The golfer		counted the flowers.
The player		shown the way.
The singer		
The hawker		
The shopkeeper		

Note: You can form as many sentences as you can but the maximum number of sentences that you can get will be 208.

19. Future Perfect Continuous

I shall	have been	crying for the payment.
We shall		trying to get it done.
She will		staying here for long.
They will		dancing on the road.
He will		begging for mercy.
The beggar will		throwing stones recklessly.
The pensioner will		getting closer.
The helper will		seeking help.
The helpless will		tearing papers.
A commoner will		

Note: You can form as many sentences as you can with the **Future Perfect Continuous Tense**, *i.e.,* **'shall or will have been'**, *but the maximum number of sentences that you can get will be 90.*

Chapter-16

Voice

A *Transitive verb* has two voices: The **Active Voice** and the **Passive Voice**. The voice of a verb shows whether the subject is the receiver of the action (passive).

Compare the following sentences: Manish helped Ravi (active)/ Ravi was helped by Manish (passive). Both sentences mean the same thing, but in the first sentence Manish (the subject) is the doer of the action (helped) and in the second sentence, Ravi (the subject) is the receiver or sufferer of the action (was helped).

Use of Passive Voice

Though the active voice is more forceful and direct, the passive voice is used in the following conditions:

When we do not want to mention the doer of the action, as:
She was found cheating.
When we do not know who is the doer of the action, as:
My pocket has been picked.
When we want to emphasize the recipient of the action, as:
The king was cheered by the people. / The old man was found dead.

Changing the Voice of a Verb

We can change a sentence from active voice to passive voice by making the following changes:
The object in the active voice is made the subject in the passive voice.
The subject in the active voice is made the object in the passive voice.
The passive form of the verb is made by adding its past participle to some form of 'be' as shown in the following points:

Simple Present Tense

He feeds pigeons. (Active)
Pigeons are fed by him. (Passive)
She teaches history. (Active)
History is taught by her. (Passive)

Simple Past Tense

A snake bit Uma.
Uma was bitten by a snake.

I wrote a poem.
A poem was written by me.

Simple Future Tense
Sasha will like this dress.
This dress will be liked by Sasha.
I shall cook dinner.
Dinner will be cooked by me.

Continuous Tense (Present and Past)
They are moving a movie.
A movie is being watched by them.
A mad dog was chasing Mona.
Mona was being chased by a mad dog.

Perfect Tense (Present, Past and Future)
He has eaten a cake.
A cake has been eaten by him.
The hunter had killed a lion.
A lion had been killed by the hunter.
The teacher will have forgiven us.
We will have been forgiven by the teacher.

Transitive Verbs Having Two Objects
When a transitive verb has two objects in the active voice, either the direct or the indirect object may become the subject in the passive voice; as,
I gave Latika a pen.
Latika was given a pen by me.
A pen was given to latika by me.
She will tell us a story.
We shall be told a story by her.
A story will be told to us by her.

Prepositional Verbs
When the verb in the active voice is a prepositional verb, the preposition is not dropped in the passive voice, as it is a part of the verb; as,
The boys laughed at the beggar.
The beggar was laughed at by the boys.
We objected to the monitor's proposal.
The monitor's proposal was objected to by us.

Auxiliary Verbs
You must do the job.
The job must be done by you.
Our team may lose the cricket match.
The cricket match may be lost by our team.

Interrogative Sentences
Has she taken a decision?
Has a decision been taken by her?
Who stole my watch?
By whom was my watch stolen?

Imperative Sentences
Shut the door.
Let the door be shut.
The door should be shut.
Let me complete my homework.
Let my homework be completed by me.

Doer of the Actions
My wallet has been stolen.
Someone has stolen my wallet.
I was obliged to leave.
Circumstances obliged me to leave.

Exercises

1. **Rewrite the following sentences according to the instructions given after each:**
   - The police caught the thief. (End: …. By the police)
   - Too much is being taken for granted. (Begin: They are….)
   - Who has broken the mirror? (Begin: By whom….)
   - They must do it at once. (End:… done at once.)
   - Someone has picked his pocket. (Begin: His pocket….)
   - Passengers are forbidden to cross the line. (End:…. Forbids passengers to cross the line)
   - Post this letter. (Begin: Let….)
   - They feel that these situations need never arise. (End:…. felt that these situations need never arise).
   - Will they help you? (End…. By them?)

2. **Without adding 'by'; change the following sentences into Passive Voice:**
   - Somebody built this orphanage last year.
   - People speak Hindi all over the world.
   - No one has ever achieved greatness without sincere efforts.
   - We called her stupid.
   - Someone has stolen his water heater.
   - People speak Assamese in Assam.
   - They don't like newcomers in this village.
   - They are serving cold drinks in the party.
   - They drank a whole jug of juice.
   - People always admire the brave.

3. **Change the voice of the following sentences:**
   - Open the window.
   - Her attitude shocked me a lot.
   - The farmers are ploughing their fields.
   - He landed the helicopter safely.
   - My mother was feeding the birds.
   - We are expecting rain.

Voice

- You should follow the advice of saints.
- Don't throw stones at the frogs.
- Take care of your health.

4. **Change the following sentences into the Active Voice. Frame at least two sentences following the pattern of each Sentence given below.**
   - Hindi is spoken in India.
   - The letter was given to me.
   - You are requested not to cry.
   - The poor should be fed.
   - The children must be loved.
   - The goods are carried by trucks.
   - Nothing is to be gained.
   - Kites were being flown.
   - He was refused admission.
   - They are being shown how to do it.
   - This matter must be looked into.
   - It is believed that the earth is round.
   - I hope to be rewarded.
   - She was paid her wages.
   - I was helped.

Chapter-1

What are Phrases and Clauses?

Read the following groups of words
On the river, of great wealth, in the bottle, every now and then, how to do it

Each of the groups of words given above conveys some idea, but does not make complete sense. Such a group of words which does not make complete sense is called **a phrase.**

A phrase has the following properties:
   a) It is a group of words.
   b) It does not have a finite verb (e.g. write, break, work, run, stop etc.), but it may contain a subject.
   c) It may contain a non-finite verb such as a participle, a gerund or an infinitive.
   d) It does not convey a definite meaning. It only conveys a disconnected idea.
   e) It cannot stand alone; it should be part of a larger sentence.

Clause

Study the following examples carefully.

He is a man of wealth.

Here the group of words 'of wealth' is a phrase because it does not contain a finite verb. It does not make complete sense either. A phrase does not have a subject or a verb.

Now read the sentence given below:

He is a man **who possesses wealth.**

Here the group of words 'who possesses wealth' contains a subject and a predicate of its own. It is therefore like a sentence.

A clause is a group of words which contains a subject and a predicate of its own. There are two kinds of clauses: **subordinate clauses and main clauses.**

A main clause can stand alone to make a sentence by itself.

Examples are given below:
- Alice started making dinner.
- Peter wrote a letter.
- Harry sang a song.

- ❑ We enjoyed the party.
- ❑ Barking dogs seldom bite.

A subordinate clause also contains a subject and a predicate of its own, but it must be attached to another clause within a larger sentence.

Read the sentence given below:

Alice worked while John played.

The sentence given above has two finite verbs. Therefore it has two clauses. Here the clause 'Alice worked' makes complete sense. It can stand alone. It is therefore **a main clause or principal clause.** Now consider the second clause 'while John played'. It does not make complete sense. In fact, it has to be attached to another clause. It is therefore a subordinate clause.

A clause has the following properties:

a) A clause is a group of words.
b) A clause has a subject and a predicate.
c) A clause has a meaning of its own.
d) A clause forms part of a larger sentence.

Exercises

1. **In each of the following sentences, replace the ADVERB in italics by an Adverb Phrase of the same meaning.**
   a. The pigeon flies *swiftly*.
      The pigeon flies _____.
   b. Did Anne behave *well*?
      Did Anne behave _____?
   c. Go *away*.
      Go _____.
   d. The dying man replied *feebly*.
      The dying man replied _____.
   e. *Gently* fell the rain.
      _____ fell the rain.
   f. We will pitch our tents *just here*.
      We will pitch our tents just _____.
   g. He expects to get promotion *soon*.
      He expects to get promotion _____.

1. **Some Exercises of Forming Sentences with Clauses**

	what I am going to tell you.
	all that I have to say.
Plan carefully	the things that must be known.
Listen to	the future plan.
Listen carefully	the actions of future.
Listen and follow	the blue print of the work chart.
Remember	what you have to do.
	what is needed now.
	what is important.
	what was discussed in the meeting.

Note: The number of sentences that you form will be 24. Also identify the type of clause in each case.

2. Form sentences and identify the type of clause in each case.

					they have done.
I	can't				they have told.
You	can	justify	what		they have achieved.
He	must	understand	that which		they have overlooked.
	must not	remind	the thing that		they have forgotten.
	should				they have borrowed.
	should not				they are overlooking.
					is important.

Note: *The number of sentences that you can get will be 756. Also identify the type of clause in each case.*

	what I am going to tell you.
	all that I have to say.
Plan carefully	the things that must be known.
Listen to	the future plan.
Listen carefully	the actions of future.
Listen and follow	the blue print of the work chart.
Remember	what you have to do.
	what is needed now.
	what is important.
	what was discussed in the meeting.

3.

He will do that	if you want.
I shall speak to him	if you ask.
You will be informed	if it is requested.
He will accept the post	if a letter is given.
They would help you	if it is offered.
He would do it	if it is proved right.
I shall oppose him	if the deadlock continues.

Note: *The maximum number of sentences that you can form will be 49.*

Chapter-2

The Sentence and Kinds of Sentences

When we speak or write we use words. We generally use these words in groups; as
Little Jack Horner sat in a corner.
A group of words which make a complete sense, is called a **sentence.**

Kinds of Sentences

Sentences are of **four kinds**:-

(1) *Those which make statements or assertions*: as**,**
Humpty Dumpty sat on a wall.

(2) *Those which ask questions*: as
Where do you live?

(3) *Those which express commands, requests, or entreaties*; as,
Be quiet, have mercy upon us.

(4) *Those which express strong feelings*; as,
How very cold the night is! What a shame!

- ❏ A sentence that makes a statement or assertion is called **a Declarative or Assertive Sentence**, as in the above, (1).
- ❏ A sentence that asks a question is called an **Interrogative Sentence,** as in the above, (2).
- ❏ A sentence that expresses a command or an entreaty is called an **Imperative Sentence**, as in the above, (3).
- ❏ A sentence that expresses strong feeling is called an **Exclamatory Sentence**, as in the above, (4).

Subject and Predicate

When we make a sentence-

(1) We name some person or thing; and
(2) Say something about that person or thing.
In other words, we must have a subject to speak and we must say or predicate something about the subject

Hence, every sentence has two parts-

(1) The part which names the person or thing we are speaking about. This is called the subject of the sentence.

(2) The part which tells something about the subject. This is called the predicate of the sentence.

The subject of a sentence usually comes first, but occasionally is put after the predicate; as:

Down went the royal George
Sweet are the uses of adversity

In Imperative Sentences, the subject is left out; as,

Sit down. (Here the subject you is understood).
Thank him, (Here too the subject you is understood).

Examine the group of words 'in a corner'. It makes sense, but not complete sense. Such group of words, which makes sense, but not complete sense, is called a **phrase**.

In the following sentences, the groups of words in italics are phrases:

The sun rises *in the east*.
There came a giant *to my door*.
It was a sunset *of great beauty*.
The tops of the mountains were covered *with snow*.
Show me *how to do it*.

Examine the groups of words in italics in the following sentences.

He has a chain *of gold*.
He has a chain which *is made of gold*.
We recognize the first group of words as a phrase.
The second group of words, unlike the phrase, *of gold*, contains a subject (which) and a predicate (*is made of gold*).
Such a group of words which forms a part of a sentence, and contains **a subject and a predicate** is called a **clause**.

In the following sentences, the groups of words in italics are clauses:

People *who pay their debts* are trusted.
We cannot start *while it is raining*.
I think *that you have made a mistake*.

1. **In the following sentences, separate the subject and the predicate.**
   - The crackling of geese saved Rome.
   - The boy stood on the burning deck.
   - Tubal Cain was a man of might.
   - Stone walls do not a prison make.
   - The singing of the birds delights us.
   - Miss kitty was rude at the table one day.
   - He has a good memory.
   - Bad habits grow unconsciously.
   - The earth revolves round the sun.
   - Nature is the best physician.

2. **Separate the subject from the predicate in the following sentences.**
   - Edison invented the phonograph.
   - The sea hath many thousand sands.
   - We cannot pump the ocean dry.
   - Borrowed garments never fit well.
   - The early bird catches the worm
   - All matter is indestructible
   - Ascham taught Latin to queen Elizabeth.
   - We should profit by experience.
   - All roads lead to Rome.
   - A guilty conscience needs no excuse.

Affirmative and Negative Sentences

1. Forming of Affirmative Sentences

Match the Sentences and frame at least two Sentences of your own following the patterns.

				they have done.
I	can't			they have told.
You	can	justify	what	they have achieved.
He	must	understand	that which	they have overlooked.
	must not	remind	the thing that	they have forgotten.
	should			they have borrowed.
	should not			they are overlooking.
				is important.

Number of Sentences that you will get = 7 + 14 = 21

2. Forming of Negative Sentences

Match the sentences and frame at least two sentences of your own following the patterns.

Are you going to work?	Yes, I am.
Can you drive a car?	Yes, I can.
Does Rita sleep well?	Yes, she does.
Did he say anything?	Yes, he did.
Is it a good film?	Yes, it is.
Sheela has already come.	So, she has.
He looks unwell.	Yes, he does.

Note: The maximum number of sentences that you will get = 7 + 14 = 21

Match the sentences. Choose from the second part to complete the sentences of the first part.

Leave the room	a limping elephant.
He failed	to be very clever.
An honest man	when she was clearing the shelf.
She always wanted	and won the match.
Luckily we	when he fared well in the interview.
We saw	to be drowned in a flooded river.
Sadly he was	and they left for the show.
She seems	to become a nurse.
She fell	at 5 a.m.

He was reported	for security reasons.
We played well	put behind the bar.
We locked the gate	escaped the accident.
The rain stopped	because he acted upon your advice.
He was appointed	is always daring.

Note: The maximum number of sentences that you can get = 14

3. Match the sentences. Choose from the second part to complete the sentences of the first part.

The Mount Everest is the highest	
January is the coldest	artist.
The Ganges is a sacred	river.
Mr. Roy is a great	game.
Ludo is the funniest	peak.
Polo is a different	month.
Nainital is a very high	
December is a very cold	
May si the hottest	
Vindhya is a famous	

Note: The maximum number of sentences that you will get = 10.

4. Choose the correct Interrogative Pronoun to complete an Interrogative Sentence. Each Interrogative Pronoun will not be suitable to each given part.

	the manager of the bank?
	the eldest sister?
Who is	I ask for help?
What is	the name of the movie?
Whom should	the longest river in Asia?
Which is	the person you are talking about?
	your preference?
	we meet first?

Note: The maximum number of sentences that you will get = 8

The Sentence and Kinds of Sentences

Chapter-3

Synthesis of Sentences

Synthesis means the combination of a number of simple sentences into one new sentence – **simple, compound** or **complex**.

The following are the chief ways of combining two or more simple sentences into one large simple sentence.

By using a participle

He sprang up to his feet. He ran away.

springing up to his feet, he ran away.

She was tired of trying. She decided to quit.

Tired (or, being tired) of trying, she decided to quit.

By using a noun or a phrase in apposition

This is my mother. Her name is Susie.

This is my mother Susie.

By using a preposition with a noun or gerund

Her husband died. She heard the news. She fainted.

On hearing the news of her husband's death she fainted.

He has failed many times. He still hopes to succeed.

In spite of many failures, he still hopes to succeed.

By using the absolute construction

The watch was expensive. He could not buy it.

The watch being expensive, he could not buy it.

The cot was too small. He could not sleep on it.

The cot being too small, he could not sleep on it.

By using an infinitive

He wanted to pass the examination. He studied hard.

He studied hard to pass the examination.

I have some duties. I must perform them.

I have some duties to perform.

By using an adverb or adverbial phrase

The sun has set. The travellers had not reached their destination.

The travellers had not reached their destination by sunset.

1. **Join the following pairs of sentences using a conjunction to form a compound sentence.**
   1. You must follow my instructions. You must resign.
   2. John couldn't have done this. Sam couldn't have done this.
   3. The burglars looted the shop. They set fire to it.
   4. He is hurt. He wants to play.
   5. He was very weak. He could barely stand.
   6. Give me the keys of the safe. You will be shot.
   7. He would not eat. He would not allow us to eat.
   8. The situation is not very difficult. People think that it is very difficult.
   9. The officer was very inefficient. He had to be sacked.
   10. The task is very difficult. You can't do it alone.

1. **Match the sentences and frame at least two sentences of your own following the patterns of each synthesised sentence.**

After burning the midnight oil	he topped in the class.
On hearing my voice	the child ran to me.
She has four children	to support.
I have much work	to do.
This is my student	Sunny.
Nehru, a famous writer	wrote the 'Discovery of India.'
Having finished this work	the workers left for home.
Being a true patriot	he will not betray his country.
In spite of being weak	he studies hard.
Frustrated with loss in business	he went mad.
While walking on the road	I saw a big dog.
Having finished his studies	he started his own agency.
Undoubtedly,	he is a great sportsman.
They had not arrived	till now.
You are taking up old issues	unnecessarily.

Note: The number of sentences that you will get= 15 + 30=45.

Synthesis of Sentences

2. Form Compound Sentences

Match the sentences and frame at least two sentences of your own following the patterns of each synthesised sentence.

We went to the University	and studied there.
She is a coward	and a fool.
Kiran is both	intelligent and beautiful.
Neither a borrower	nor a lender be.
Either Rajan or Ravi	will have to face the situation.
Word hard	else you will fail.
Either pay the price	or return the pen.
I know Mohan	but not Ravi.
Though, I rebuked him	yet he kept mum.
Although, he lost his position	nevertheless, he kept his cool.
I don't believe in what you say	however, I shall not oppose you.
She stood first in the class	therefore, she was given a prize.
I can't depend on him	for he is a fool.
He is definitely	talented and diligent.

Note: The maximum number of sentences you will get = 14 + 28= 32.

3 Form Complex Sentences

Match the sentences and frame at least two sentences of your own following the patterns of each synthesised sentence.

Everyone knows it	that he is an honest boy.
The fact that Bose was a great scientist	can not be challenged.
Ask him	why he is late.
I can not understand	what you say.
He is the boy	who stood first in his class.
This is the book	which he gave me.
They want a mechanic	who repairs computers.
This is the girl	whom her mother is calling.

Note: The maximum number of sentences formed will be 8 + 16=24.

Chapter-4

Transformation of Sentences

Transformation is changing the form of a sentence without changing its meaning. In the exams transformation should be done according to the direction given in the question paper. In doing transformation a student should have a fairly well knowledge about the kinds of sentence and their formation. A brief direction about doing transformation is given below.

Affirmative to Negative:

Rule 1: Only/ alone/ merely → Replaced by → None but (person)/ nothing but(things)/ not more than or not less than(number)

    Eg. Affirmative: Only Allah can help us. Negative: None but Allah can help us.

Affirmative: He has only a ball. Negative: He has nothing but a ball.

Affirmative: He has only ten rupees. Negative: He has not more than ten rupees.

Rule 2: Must → Replaced by → Cannot but/ Cannot help+ (v+ing).

    Eg. Affirmative: We must obey our parents. Negative: We cannot but obey our parents/We cannot help obeying our parents.

Rule 3: Both----and → Replaced by → not only ---- but also.

    Ex: Aff: Both Dolon and Dola were excited.

    Neg: Not only dolon but also Dola were present.

Rule 4: and (if join two words) → Replaced by → Not only ----- but also.

    Ex: aff: He was obedient and gentle. Neg: He was not only obedient but also gentle.

Rule 5: Everyone/ everybody/every person/ (every + common noun)/all → Replaced by → There is no + attached word + but.

    Ex: Aff: Every mother loves her child.

    Neg: There is no mother but loves her child.

Rule 6: As soon as → Replaced by → No sooner had ----- Than.

    Ex: Aff: As soon as the thief saw the police, he ran away. Neg: No sooner had the thief saw the police he ran away.

Rule 7: Absolute Superlative degree → Replaced by → No other+ attached word+so+ positive form+ as+subject.

    Ex: aff: Dhaka is the biggest city in Bangladesh.

    Neg: No other city is as big as Dhaka in Bangladesh.

Rule 8: Sometimes affirmative sentences are changed into negative by using opposite words. Before the word, off course 'not' is used.

    Ex: Aff: I shall remember you. Neg: I shall not forget you.

Rule 9: Always → Replaced by → Never.

Ex: aff: Raven always attends the class. Neg: Raven never misses the class.

Rule 10: Too ---- to → Replaced by → so ---that+ can not/could not(in past).

Ex: Aff: He is too weak to walk. Neg: He is so weak that he cannot walk.

Rule 11: As – as → Replaced by → Not less – than.

Ex: Aff: Simi was as wise as Rimi. Neg: Simi was not less wise than Rimi.

Rule 12: Universal truth are change by making them negative interrogative.

Ex: Aff: The Sun sets in the west. Neg: Doesn't the Sun set in the west?

Rule 13: Sometimes → Replaced by → Not + always.

Ex: Aff: Raven sometimes visits me. Neg: Raven doesn't always visit me.

Rule 14: Many → Replaced by → Not a few.

Ex: Aff: I have many friends. Neg: I donot have few friends.

Rule 15: A few → Replaced by → not many.

Ex: Aff: Bangladesh has a few scholars. Neg: Bangladesh doesn't have many scholars.

Rule 16: Much → Replaced by → A little.

Ex: Aff: He belongs much money. Neg: He doesn't belong a little money.

Rule 17: A little → Replaced by → not much.

Ex: Aff: Dolon has a little riches. Neg: Dolon doesn't have much riches.

Assertive to Interrogative

Rule 1: If the sentence is in the affirmative you have to change it into negative interrogative. If it is in negative then you have to change it into bare interrogative.

Ex: Ass: He was very gentle.

Int: was n't he very gentle?

Aff: He is not a good person.

Int: Is he a good person?

Rule 2: No auxiliary verb in sentence →→ Change it by using →→ Do/does/did or Don't/doesn't/didn't.

Ex: Ass:He plays Football.

Int: Does he play football?

Ass: They did not play football yesterday.

Int: Did they play football yesterday?

Rule 3: Never → Replaced by → Ever.

Ass: I never drink tea.

Int: Do I ever drink tea?

Rule 4: Everybody/everyone/ All → Replaced by → Who + Don't/ Doesn't/ Didn't

Ex: Everybody wishes to be happy.

Int : Who doesn't wish to be happy?

Rule 5: Every + noun → Replaced by → Is there any + noun+ Who don't/doesn't/didn't.

Ex: Ass: Every man wishes to be happy.
Int: Is there any man who doesn't wish to be happy?

Rule 6: No body/ no one / None → Replaced by → Who.

Ex: Nobody could count my love for you.
Int: Who could ever count my love for you?

Rule 7: There is no → Replaced by → Is there any/ Who(person)/ What(thing).

Ex: Ass: There is no use of this law.
Int: What is the use of this law.
Ass: There is no man happier than Jamil.
Int: Who is Happier than jamil.

Rule 8: It Is no → Replaced by → Is there any/Why.

Ex: Ass: It is no use of taking unfair means in the exam.
Int: Why take unfair means in the exam? Or,
Is there any use of this law?

Rule 9: It Doesn't matter → Replaced by → what though/ Does it matter.

Ex: Ass: It does not matter if you fail in te exam.
Int: What though if you fail in the exam?
Interrogative to assertive is to be done doing vice versa.

Exclamatory to Assertive

Rule1: Subject and Verb of exclamatory sentence are to be used as the subject and verb of assertive sentence at the outset of the sentence.

How/what → Replace by → Very(before adjective)/ Great(before noun)
Ex: How fortunate you are!
Ass: You are very fortunate.
Exc: What a fool you are!
Ass: You are a great fool.

Rule 2: Sometimes the subject and verb may be eclipsed.

Ex: What a beautiful scenery!
Ass: It is a very beautiful scenery.
Ex: What a pity!
Ass: It is a great pity.

Rule 3: Hurrah/ Bravo → Replace by → I/we rejoice that/ It is a matter of joy that.

Ex: Hurrah! We have own the game.
Ass: It is a matter of joy that we have won the game.

Rule 4: Alas → Replace by → I/we Mourn that/ It is a matter of sorrow or grief that.

Ex: Alas! He has failed.
Ass: We mourn that he has failed.

Rule 5: Had/were/If /Would that (at the outset) → Replaced by → I wish + subject again + were/ had+ rest part.

Ex: Had I the wings of a bird!
Ass: I wish I had the wings of a bird.
Ex: Were I a bird!
Ass: I wish I were a bird.
Ex: If I were young again!
Ass: I wish I were young again.
Ex: Would that I could be a child!
Ass: I wish I could be a child.

Assertive to Exclamatory is to be done doing the vice versa of the above.

Imperative to Assertive

Rule 1: Add subject + should in doing assertive.

Ex: Do the work.
Ass: You should do the work.

Rule 2: Please/kindly → Replaced by →You are requested to.

Ex: Please, help me.
Ass: You are requested to help me.

Rule 3: Do not → Replaced by → You should not.

Ex: Do not run in the sun.
Ass: You should not run in the sun.

Rule 4: Never → Replaced by → you should never.

Ex: Never tell a lie.
Ass: You should never tell a lie.

Rule 5: Let us → Replaced by → We should.

Ex: Let us go out for a walk.
Ass: We should go out for a walk.

Rule 6: Let + noun/pronoun → Replaced by → Subject + might.

Ex: Let him play football.
Ass: He might play football.

Sentences having the Adverb, 'Too'

The dog is too old to learn new things.
The dog is so old that it cannot learn new things.
He is too clever not to see through your tricks.
He is so clever that he sees through your tricks.

Interchanging of Degrees of Comparison
- He runs as fast as a deer. (Positive)
- A deer does not run faster than he. (Comparative)
- Hydrogen is the lightest of all gases. (Superlative)
- Hydrogen is lighter than any other gas. (Comparative)
- No gas is as light as hydrogen. (Positive)

Interchange of Active and Passive Voice
- I wrote a poem. (Active)
- A poem was written by me. (Passive)
- Who taught you French? (Active)
- By whom was French taught to you? (Passive)

Interchange of Parts of Speech
- *Noun:* The patient put up a brave fight.
- *Verb:* The patient fought bravely.
- *Noun:* It was her intention to tease me.
- *Adverb*: She teased me intentionally.

Interchange of Principal and Subordinate Clauses
- He is so weak that he cannot walk.
- He cannot walk as he is very weak.
- It never rains but pours.
- It always pours when it rains.

1. **Conversion of simple sentences into compound sentences**
   Simple: The weather being fine, we went out for a walk.
   Compound: The weather was fine and we went out for a walk.
   Simple: Notwithstanding her old age, my mother works hard.
   Compound: My mother is old but she works hard.

2. **Conversion of compound sentences into simple sentences**
   Compound: He is poor, but he is happy.
   Simple: In spite of his poverty, he is happy.
   Simple: You must work hard to pass the examination.
   Compound: The sun rose and the fog dispersed.
   Simple: The sun having risen, the fog dispersed.

3. **Conversion of compound sentences into complex sentences**
   Compound: Run fast, or you will miss the train.
   Complex: Unless you run fast, you will miss the train.

Transformation of Sentences

Compound: He will come today and I have no doubt about it.
Complex: I have no doubt that he will come today.

4. **Conversion of complex sentences into compound sentences**
   Complex: I have found the ring that I have lost.
   Compound: I have lost her ring, but I have found it.
   Complex: If you do not hurry you will miss the train.
   Compound: You must hurry, or you will miss the train.

5. **Conversion of simple sentences into complex sentences**

   NOUN CLAUSES
   - Simple: No one can foretell the time of his death.
   - Complex: No one can foretell when he will die.
   - Simple: Her ambition was to become a doctor.
   - Complex: Her ambition was that she should become a doctor.

   ADJECTIVE CLAUSES
   - Simple: All glittering things are not gold.
   - Complex: All that glitters is not gold.
   - Simple: A man in danger needs help.
   - Complex: A man who is in danger needs help.

   ADVERB CLAUSES
   - Simple: We eat to live.
   - Complex: We eat so that we may live.
   - Simple: I will go with your permission.
   - Complex: I will go if you give me permission.

Exercises

1. **Interchange the principal and the subordinate clauses in the following sentences:**
   - Look before you leap.
   - As soon as the storm began, the boat capsized.
   - Unless you work hard, you will not come up in life.
   - He never makes a promise which he cannot keep.
   - He ran away as soon as he saw me.
   - I cannot speak loudly because I have a sore throat.
   - I was so foolish that I did not act upon my teacher's advice.
   - She does not like him because he is proud.
   - No sooner did the bell ring than the boys ran into their classes.
   - The money was not returned until the thief was beaten.

Chapter-5

Direct and Indirect Speech

There are two ways of relating what a person has said. We may quote his actual words. This is called direct speech. We may report what he said without quoting his exact words. This is called indirect speech.

He said, "I am busy now."(Direct)
He said that he was busy then. (Indirect)

Direct Speech

The actual words of a speaker are put within inverted commas. (" ")
The first word of a reported speech begins with a capital letter.
The reported speech is separated by a comma from the reporting verb.

Indirect Speech

Inverted commas are not used, but the conjunction 'that' is used
The comma separating the reporting verb from the reported speech is removed.
The tense of the reporting verb is never changed.
The question mark and the exclamatory mark are not used.
Interrogative imperative and exclamatory sentences are put as statements.

Assertive Sentences

Assertive sentences in the indirect speech are usually introduced by the conjunction 'that':
They said to Anuj, "you are a brave boy."
They told Anuj that he was a brave boy.

The verbs tell, inform, remind and assure always take a personal object after them, hence the form said to me is changed generally into told me and sometimes into informed me, reminded me, or assured me, as the sense may require; as,

The teacher said to me," I have never seen such a lazy girl as you are."
The teacher told me that she had never seen such a lazy girl as I was.

Imperative Sentences

When the direct speech is an imperative mood, the reporting verb say or tell is changed to some verb expressing a command, advice or request.

The imperative mood is changed into the infinitive.
The rules for the change of pronouns are to be observed.

That is generally not used. If it is used, then should is placed before the imperative instead of 'to'
When let in the direct speech expresses a proposal or suggestion, you may use should and change the reporting verb into propose or suggest; as,

- ❏ Direct: He said to us, "let us have some coffee."
- ❏ Indirect: He proposed to us that we should have some coffee.
- ❏ Direct: The teacher said to the pupils, "Do not stand here."
- ❏ Indirect: the teacher forbade the students to stand there.

Exclamatory Sentences

In reporting a wish or an exclamation in the indirect speech:

The reporting verb say or tell is changed into wish bless, pray, cry, exclaim, declare, confess, cry out etc., with such phrases as with regret with delight or joy with sorrow where necessary.

- ❏ Direct: He said, "God save my son!"
- ❏ Indirect: He prayed that God might save his son.
- ❏ Direct : "What a horrible accident it is!" he said.
- ❏ Indirect: He exclaimed that it was a horrible accident.

Interrogative Sentences

In reporting a question in the indirect speech:

The reporting verb is changed to asked, inquired, demanded. Etc.

The note of interrogation which is placed after questions in the direct form is replaced by a full stop.

- ❏ Direct: He said to me, "Do you know the way?"
- ❏ Indirect: He inquired of me if I knew the way.

1. **Rewrite the following in Direct Speech:**
   - ❑ The boy asked me how old I was.
   - ❑ The stranger asked Ashish where he lived.
   - ❑ Ramu asked Nitin whether he had made a mistake.
   - ❑ They asked me what I wanted.
   - ❑ The young mouse asked who would bell the cat.
   - ❑ I asked Nihal if he would lend me a pen.
   - ❑ The policeman inquired of the girl where she was going.
   - ❑ She enquired of us whether we were playing football.

1. **Form ten sentences of Direct Speech. Subject + Verb+ Direct Object + Preposition + Prepositional Object**

Thank	You	for	your kind help.
Ask	him	for	a few more.
Compare	this	with	that flag.
They punished	him	for	being very late.
Congratulate	him	on	his grand success.
Do not throw	the stone	at	the poor donkey.
What prevented	you	from	joining the post?
Add	this	to	what you have.
I explained	my difficulty	to	the manager.
Protect	us	from	the terrorists.

Note: The maximum number of sentences that you will get is 10.

2. **Form Indirect Sentences. Subject + Verb + Indirect Object + Direct Object**

Subject + Verb	Indirect Object	Direct Object
Have they paid	You	the subscription?
Will you lend	me	your book?

Did our teacher give	us	home work?
Did I read	him	the newspaper?
Please throw	me	a pen.
His grand father told	him	a nice story.
He handed	me	the cheque.
The pupils wished	the teachers	'Happy New Year.'
He denies	her	nothing essential.

Note: The maximum number of sentences that you will get is 9.

Chapter-6

Punctuation

Punctuation marks are symbols that indicate the structure and organization of written language, as well as intonation and pauses to be observed when reading aloud.

In written English, punctuation is vital to disambiguate the meaning of sentences. For example, "woman, without her man, is nothing" (emphasizing the importance of men) and "woman: without her, man is nothing" (emphasising the importance of women) have greatly different meanings, as do "eats shoots and leaves" (to mean "consumes plant growths") and "eats, shoots and leaves" (to mean "eats firstly, fires a weapon secondly, and leaves the scene thirdly").[1]

The rules of punctuation vary with language, location, register and time and are constantly evolving. Certain aspects of punctuation are stylistic and are thus the author's (or editor's) choice. Tachygraphic language forms, such as those used in online chat and text messages, may have wildly different rules. For English usage, see the articles on specific punctuation marks.

History

Punctuation developed dramatically when large numbers of copies of the Christian Bible started to be produced. These were designed to be read aloud and the copyists began to introduce a range of marks to aid the reader, including indentation, various punctuation marks and an early version of initial capitals. Saint Jerome and his colleagues, who produced the Vulgate translation of the Bible into Latin, developed an early system (circa 400 AD); this was considerably improved on by Alcuin. The marks included the virgule (forward slash) and dots in different locations; the dots were centred in the line, raised or in groups.

With the invention of moveable type in Europe began an increase of printed material. "The rise of printing in the 14th and 15th centuries meant that a standard system of punctuation was urgently required." The introduction of a standard system of punctuation has also been attributed to Aldus Manutius and his grandson. They have been credited with popularizing the practice of ending sentences with the colon or full stop, inventing the semicolon, making occasional use of parentheses and creating the modern comma by lowering the virgule. By 1566, Aldus Manutius the Younger was able to state that the main object of punctuation was the clarification of syntax.

By the 19th century, punctuation in the western world had evolved "to classify the marks hierarchically, in terms of weight". Cecil Hartley's poem identifies their relative values:

The stop point out, with truth, the time of pause

A sentence doth require at ev'ry clause.

At ev'ry comma, stop while one you count;

At semicolon, two is the amount;

A colon doth require the time of three;

The period four, as learned men agree.

The use of punctuation was not standardised until after the invention of printing. According to the 1885 edition of The American Printer, the importance of punctuation was noted in various sayings by children such as:

Charles the First walked and talked

Half an hour after his head was cut off.

With a semi-colon and a comma added it reads:

Charles the First walked and talked;

Half an hour after, his head was cut off.

Shortly after the invention of printing, the necessity of stops or pauses in sentences for the guidance of the reader produced the colon and full point. In process of time, the comma was added, which was then merely a perpendicular line, proportioned to the body of the letter. These three points were the only ones used until the close of the fifteenth century, when Aldo Manuccio gave a better shape to the comma, and added the semicolon; the comma denoting the shortest pause, the semicolon next, then the colon, and the full point terminating the sentence. The marks of interrogation and admiration were introduced many years after.

The standards and limitations of evolving technologies have exercised further pragmatic influences. For example, minimisation of punctuation in typewritten matter became economically desirable in the 1960s and 1970s for the many users of carbon-film ribbons, since a period or comma consumed the same length of expensive non-reusable ribbon as did a capital letter.

Conventional Styles of English Punctuation

There are two major styles of punctuation in English: American or traditional punctuation; and British or logical punctuation. These two styles differ mainly in the way in which they handle quotation marks.

Arabic, Urdu, and Persian languages—written from right to left—use a reversed question mark: ؟, and a reversed comma: ، . This is a modern innovation; pre-modern Arabic did not use punctuation. Hebrew, which is also written from right to left, uses the same characters as in English, "," and "?".

Originally, Sanskrit had no punctuation. In the 17th century, Sanskrit and Marathi, both written in the Devanagari script, started using the vertical bar (|) to end a line of prose and double vertical bars (||) in verse.

Texts in Chinese, Japanese, and Korean were generally left unpunctuated until the modern era. In unpunctuated texts, the grammatical structure of sentences in classical writing is inferred from context. Most punctuation marks in modern Chinese, Japanese, and Korean have similar functions to their English counterparts; however, they often look different and have different customary rules.

Novel Punctuation Marks

"Love point" and similar marks

In 1966, the French author Hervé Bazin proposed a series of six innovative punctuation marks in his book Plumons l'Oiseau ("Let's pluck the bird", 1966).[11] Besides a ψ-shaped irony mark (point d'ironie), these were:[12]

the "love point" (point d'amour: Point d'amour.svg)

the "certitude point" (point de conviction: Point de certitude.svg)

the "authority point" (point d'autorité: Point d'autorité.svg)

the "acclamation point" (point d'acclamation: Point d'acclamation.svg)

the "doubt point" (point de doute: Point de doute.svg)

"question comma", "exclamation comma"

An international patent application was filed, and published in 1992 under WO number WO9219458, for two new punctuation marks: the "question comma" and the "exclamation comma". The patent application entered into national phase exclusively with Canada, advertised as lapsing in Australia on 27 January 1994 and in Canada on 6 November 1995.

Exercises

This exercise will test your understanding of all kinds of different punctuation marks, particularly, *commas, colons, semi-colons and apostrophes.*

Select the correctly punctuated sentence by putting a tick mark _____ on the right one.

1. a) Spain is a beautiful country; the beache's are warm, sandy and spotlessly clean.
   b) Spain is a beautiful country: the beaches are warm, sandy and spotlessly clean.
   c) Spain is a beautiful country, the beaches are warm, sandy and spotlessly clean.
   d) Spain is a beautiful country; the beaches are warm, sandy and spotlessly clean.

2. a) The children's books were all left in the following places: Mrs Smith's room, Mr. Powell's office and the caretaker's cupboard.
   b) The children's books were all left in the following places; Mrs Smith's room, Mr Powell's office and the caretaker's cupboard.
   c) The childrens books were all left in the following places: Mrs Smiths room, Mr Powells office and the caretakers cupboard.
   d) The children's books were all left in the following places, Mrs Smith's room, Mr Powell's office and the caretaker's cupboard.

3. a) She always enjoyed sweets, chocolate, marshmallows and toffee apples.
   b) She always enjoyed: sweets, chocolate, marshmallows and toffee apples.
   c) She always enjoyed sweets chocolate marshmallows and toffee apples.
   d) She always enjoyed sweet's, chocolate, marshmallow's and toffee apple's.

4. a) Sarah's uncle's car was found without its wheels in that old derelict warehouse.
   b) Sarah's uncle's car was found without its wheels in that old, derelict warehouse.
   c) Sarahs uncles car was found without its wheels in that old, derelict warehouse.
   d) Sarah's uncle's car was found without it's wheels in that old, derelict warehouse.

5. a) I can't see Tim's car, there must have been an accident.
   b) I cant see Tim's car; there must have been an accident.
   c) I can't see Tim's car there must have been an accident.
   d) I can't see Tim's car; there must have been an accident.

Punctuation

6. a) Paul's neighbours were terrible; so his brother's friends went round to have a word.
   b) Paul's neighbours were terrible: so his brother's friends went round to have a word.
   c) Paul's neighbours were terrible, so his brother's friends went round to have a word.
   d) Paul's neighbours were terrible so his brother's friends went round to have a word.
7. a) Tims gran, a formidable woman, always bought him chocolate, cakes, sweets and a nice fresh apple.
   b) Tim's gran a formidable woman always bought him chocolate, cakes, sweets and a nice fresh apple.
   c) Tim's gran, a formidable woman, always bought him chocolate cakes sweets and a nice fresh apple.
   d) Tim's gran, a formidable woman, always bought him chocolate, cakes, sweets and a nice fresh apple.
8. a) After stealing Tims car, the thief lost his way and ended up the chief constable's garage.
   b) After stealing Tim's car the thief lost his way and ended up the chief constable's garage.
   c) After stealing Tim's car, the thief lost his way and ended up the chief constable's garage.
   d) After stealing Tim's car, the thief lost his' way and ended up the chief constable's garage.
9. a) We decided to visit: Spain, Greece, Portugal and Italy's mountains.
   b) We decided to visit Spain, Greece, Portugal and Italys mountains.
   c) We decided to visit Spain, Greece, Portugal and Italy's mountains.
   d) We decided to visit Spain Greece Portugal and Italy's mountains.
10. a) That tall man, Paul's grandad, is this month's winner.
    b) That tall man Paul's grandad is this month's winner.
    c) That tall man, Paul's grandad, is this months winner.
    d) That tall man, Pauls grandad, is this month's winner.

Chapter-7

Verb Patterns: Sentence Structure: Syntax

Write the sentences of all the following tables and construct a minimum of Five Sentences on the pattern of each sentence of each table.

1. Subject + Verb + Direct Object

Subject + Verb	Direct Object
He cut	his finger.
We have already had	breakfast.
He does not like	cold weather.
We always	do that.
I want	six.
We lit	a fire.
They were throwing	stones.
A baby cannot dress	itself.
He laughed	a merry laugh.
She smiled	her thanks
I dug	a hole.

Note: The maximum number of sentences that you can form will be 10+50=60

2. Subject + Verb + to/ not to + Infinite etc.

Subject + Verb	(not) + to + Infinite etc
He wants	to go.
I have promised	to help them.
They decided	to go.
Did you remember	to close the window?
I agreed	to pay for it.
Have you	to go to school today?
Would you care	to go for walk?
He pretended	not to see me.

Note: The maximum number of sentences that you can form will be 8+ 40=48

3. Subject + Verb + Noun/ Pronoun + to/ not to + Infinite, etc.

Subject + Verb	Noun/ Pronoun	to/ not to + Infinite etc
He wants	me	to be early.
I asked	him	not to do it.
I told	the servant	to open the window.
Please help	me	to carry this box.
He likes	his wife	to dress well.
Your teachers expects	you	to work hard.
I warned	him	not to be late.
He allowed	the soldiers	to take him prisoner.
They have never known	him	to behave so well.

Note: The maximum number of sentences that you can get = 9 + 45 + 9 = 63. Also make in passive form, i.e., He was warned not to be late.

4. Subject + Verb + Noun/ Pronoun + (to be) + Complement

Subject + Verb	Noun/ Pronoun	(to be)	Complement
They believed	him	(to be will be used in passive only)	innocent.
Do you consider	her		laborious?
I feel	it		unhealthy.
His mother	him		a clever boy.
We proved	him		wrong.

Note: The maximum number of sentences that you can get = 5 + 5

Make in passive form too:

He was believed innocent, or

He was believed to be innocent.

Is she considered laborious?

Is she considered to be laborious?

5. Subject + Verb + Noun/ Pronoun + Infinitive etc.

Subject + Verb	Noun/ Pronoun	Infinitive etc
She will have	him	do the work.
She heard	him	go out.
We saw	them	come in.
They felt	the bus	moving.
Watch	me	do it.

Did you notice	the thief	leave the house.
She made	him	work hard.
Let	them	go.
Don't let	the matter	aggravate.
They will help	me	carry this load.
Would you have	me	believe that?
We have never known	him	behave so badly.

Note: The maximum number of sentences which you can form = 12 + 12

Make in the passive form also:

He was made to work hard.

The bus was felt moving.

6. Subject + Verb + Noun/ Pronoun + Present Participle

Subject + Verb	Noun/ Pronoun	Present Participle
We watched	the train	leaving the station.
Do you feel	the house	shaking?
Can you smell	something	burning?
I saw	him	tumbling down.
He kept	me	waiting.
I found	him	working late.
They left	me	alone.
I heard	her	weeping.

Note: The maximum number of sentences that you can form will be 8 + 8
Make in passive form too:

I was kept waiting.

She was heard weeping.

7. Subject + Verb + Object + Adjective

Subject + Verb	Object	Adjective
Do not get	your books	torn.
The moon keeps	the nights	cool.
Don't make	yourself	lazy.
Get	the room	furnished.
I found	the box	missing.
He painted	the gate	blue.
They set	the bird	free.

Verb Patterns: Sentence Structure: Syntax

Please push	the door	open.
Winter turned	the leaves	yellow.
The doctor found	the patient	dead.

Note: The maximum number of sentences that you can form will be 10 + 10

Change them into Passive Voice:

The box was found missing.

The gate was painted blue.

The bird was set free.

8. Subject + Verb + Object + Noun

Subject + Verb	Object	Noun
We elected	him	president.
The team crowned	him	captain.
The board chose	Mr. Gupta	Managing Director.
He named	the house	'Heaven'.
The parents call	their son	Umang.
The win made	the captain	hero.
The management declared	her	Principal.
They made	the clerk	manager.

Note: The maximum number of sentences that you can form = 8 + 8

Change into Passive Voice:

The house was named 'Heaven'.

She was declared principal.

9. Subject + Verb + Object + Past Participle

Subject + Verb	Object	Past Participle
She must get	her hair	cleaned.
Where did you get	them	posted?
Has she	a new car	bought?
Have you ever heard	Samskrit	recited?
His book has	a reward	Fetched.
The police had	a criminal	encountered.
Why did you get	them	printed?
Has he	his new book	Given?

Note: The maximum number of sentences that you can form = 8

10. Subject + Verb + Object + Adverb/Adverbial Phrase

Subject + Verb	Object	Adverb/ Adverbial Phrase
They treat	the girl	as if a maid.
He takes	a day	off.
Put	the book	here.
I don't know	him	to speak to.
They led	me	to feel safe.
They invited	the groom	to meet the bride.
He went to	the clinic	as advised by the doctor.
She performed	a solo	to raise money.
He has given	it	away.
They brought	the girl	to see me.
He showed	me	to the car.

Note: The maximum number of sentences that you can get = 11

11. Subject + Verb + Noun/ Pronoun + (that) Clause

Subject + Verb	(that) Clause
I hope	(that) you will come.
I suppose	(that) you will be there.
He explained	(that) nothing could be done.
Do you think	(that) it will rain?
He saw	(that) the plan was useless.
I suggest	(that) he should leave early.

Note: The maximum number of sentences that you can form will be 6 + 6
Change into Passive on the pattern given below:
It was explained that nothing could be done.
It was seen that the plan was useless.

12. Subject + Verb + Noun/ Pronoun + (that) Clause

Subject + Verb	(that) Clause
I hope	(that) you will come.
I suppose	(that) you will be there.
He explained	(that) nothing could be done.
Do you think	(that) it will rain?
He saw	(that) the plan was useless.
I suggest	(that) he should leave early.

Note: The maximum number of sentences that you can get = 4

13. Subject + Verb + Conjunctive + to Infinitive

Subject + Verb	Conjunctive	to Infinitive
I wonder	how	To do it.
I do not know	what	to do.
He is learning	how	to swim.
She was wondering	which	to buy.
Will you find out	how	to get there.
You must remember	when	to begin.
I do not know	whether	to go or stay.

Note: The maximum number of sentences that you form = 7

14. Subject + Verb + Noun/ Pronoun + Conjunctive + to Infinitive

Subject + Verb	Noun/ Pronoun	Conjunctive	to Infinitive
We showed	him	how	to do it.
Please tell	me	which	to take.
Can you advise	me	which	to buy?
The patterns show	you	how	to make sentences.
Tell	me	whether	to come or not.
They told	him	when	to start.
Tell	her	what	to do.

Number of sentences   7 + 7

Change into Passive Voice on the pattern given below:

He was showed how to do it.

He was told when to start.

15. Subject + Verb + Conjunctive + Clause

Subject + Verb	Conjunctive	Clause
I wonder	why	he has not come.
I wonder	whether / if	he will come.
I do not mind	where	we go.
Do you know	who	he is?
I do not care	what	you think.
Can you suggest	where	this ought to go?
Please say	what	you want.
Nobody says	whose	It is.

Number of sentences   8

16. Subject + Verb

Subject + Verb	Noun/ Pronoun	Conjunctive	Clause
Tell	me	what	it is.
Ask	him	where	he put it.
They asked	us	when	we should be back.
Can you tell	me	how	high it is?
Can you inform	me	when	the train leaves.
Please advise	me	when	these seeds should be sown.

Number of sentences 6

17. Subject + Verb + Gerund

Subject + Verb	Gerund
Please stop	talking.
He enjoys	playing tennis.
I remember	doing it.
Please excuse	me being so late.
Do you mind	staying a little longer?
Do you mind	my staying a little longer?
She could not	laughing.
He keeps on	coming here.
They went on	talking.
Has it left off	raining yet.

Number of sentences 10

18. Subject + Verb + Gerund, etc.

Combine each of the first part with each of the second part to frame separate sentences.

Subject + Verb	Gerund
Please stop	talking.
Subject + Verb	Gerund, etc.
He began	talking./ to talk.
He likes	swimming./ to swim.
I prefer	staying indoors./ to stay indoors.
I hate	refusing every time./ to refuse every time.
He started	packing books./ to pack his books.

Number of sentences   25 + 25

19. Subject + Verb + Gerund, etc.

Combine each of the first part with each of the second part, to frame separate sentences.

Subject + Verb	Gerund etc (Passive Infinite)
It wants	elaborating. / to be elaborated.
Your work needs	correcting. / to be corrected.
That needs	explaining. / to be explained.
He needs	refreshing. / to be refreshed.

    Number of sentences   16 + 16

20. Subject + Verb + Direct Object + Preposition + Prepositional Object

Subject + Verb		Preposition	
I gave	the money	to	my friend.
They told	the news	to	everybody they met.
We showed	the pictures	to	our teachers.
I do not lend	my books	to	anybody.
He offered	once	to	me.
I owe	thirty rupees	to	my tailor.
Throw	that box	to	me.
Bring	that book	to	me.

    Number of sentences   8

21. Subject + Verb+ Direct Object + Preposition + Prepositional Object

Subject + Verb	Direct Object	Preposition	Prepositional object
He bought	a necklace	for	the bride.
He gifted	a gold watch	to	his wife.
Please give	some	for	me.
They left	a message	for	the commander.
She made	a new dress	for	herself.
Have you left	any	for	your sister.
Please get	two tickets	for	me.
They selected	a bride	for	their son.

    Number of sentences   8

22. Subject + Verb+ Direct Object + Preposition + Prepositional Object

Subject + Verb	Direct Object	Preposition	Prepositional Object
Thank	you	for	your kind help.
Ask	him	for	a few more.

Compare	this	with	that flag.
They punished	him	for	being very late.
Congratulate	him	on	his grand success.
Do not throw	the stone	at	the poor donkey.
What prevented	you	from	joining the post?
Add	this	to	what you have.
I explained	my difficulty	to	the manager.
Protect	us	from	the terrorists.

Number of sentences 10

23. Subject + Verb + Indirect Object + Direct Object

Subject + Verb	Indirect Object	Direct Object
Have they paid	you	the subscription?
Will you lend	me	your book?
Did our teacher give	us	home work?
Did I read	him	the newspaper?
Please throw	me	a pen.
His grand father told	him	a nice story.
He handed	me	the cheque.
The pupils wished	the teachers	'Happy New Year.'
He denies	her	nothing essential.

Number of sentences 9

24. Subject + Verb + Indirect Object + Direct Object

Subject + Verb	Indirect Object	Direct Object
She made	herself	a nice bag.
Her father bought	me	a new dress.
Please buy	me	a cup of tea.
Did you leave	her	a message?
She ordered	him	a pass.
Will you do	her	a favour?
Can you spare	me	a bed for the night?
Can you get	me	a ticket for me?

Number of sentences 8

Verb Patterns: Sentence Structure: Syntax

25. Subject + Verb + Direct Object I + Direct Object II

Subject + Verb	Direct Object I	Direct Object II
Forgive	him	his childish behaviour.
They asked	me	the secret.
They smeared	me	ink.
They saved	me	a great deal of trouble.
I envy	you	for the fine house.
Forgive	us	our mistakes.
That will save	me	some money.
I struck	him	a heavy blow.
I gave	him	an upper cut.
He asked	me	a question.

Number of sentences 10

26. Subject + Verb + (for) Complement

Subject + Verb	(for) Complement
We walked	(for) five kilometers.
They had come	a long way.
The forest stretched	(for) miles and miles.
The rain lasted	all day long.
He may live	(for) many more years.
They waited	(for) four hours.
The temperature rose	five degrees.
It weighs	eighty kilograms.
It costs	One thousand.
Will she stay	(for) the night?

Number of sentences   13

27. Subject + Verb

Subject	Verb
Fire	burns.
Birds	flew.
We all	eat, drink, breathe and sleep.
The moon	shines.
The sun	rose.
A cat	jumped.

Bees	fly.
Boys	play.
A child	cried.
A writer	writes.

Number of sentences 10

28. Subject + Verb

Predicative is that part of a general sentence that follows the verb and gives information about the subject of the sentence. It (the Predicative) may be an Adjective, Adjective Phrase, Noun or Pronoun.

Subject + Verb	Predicative
This is	a table.
This box	is yours.
That will be	enough.
Please get	to receive her.
The weather has become	colder.
The leaves have turned	yellow.
It feels	smooth and cold.
The plan proved	a boon.
The results are	quite unexpected.
His dream came	true.
The curd turned	sour.

Number of sentences   11

Note: *This Verb Pattern is used in various ways with slight variations. The following are some variants of this Verb Pattern. Frame at least five sentences on each of these patterns.*

   a. With Preparatory it: e.g.
- It is easy to say so.
- It is a pity he could not pass.
- It is no use your trying to mend it.
- It would be sad to waste it.

   b. With an Infinitive Phrase as complement: e.g.
- This shop is to let.
- To see her is to appreciate her.
- My aim is to encourage the students.

c. **With the subject complement first: e.g.**
- ❑ What is that?
- ❑ What are you holding?
- ❑ What price is that suit?

d. **With an Adverb or Prepositional Phrase as the complement: e.g.**
- ❑ She is in good mood.
- ❑ The car is out of order.
- ❑ The boy is out of control.
- ❑ The fruit is far too ripe.

29. Subject + Verb

Subject + Verb	Adverbial Adjunct
Stand	up!
Sit	down!
Turn	back!
The sun sets	in the west.
We did not go	anywhere.
He will go	as soon as he is ready.
I will help	as much as practicable.
A piece of furniture will not stand	on two legs.

Number of sentences 8

30. Subject + Verb + Preposition + Prepositional Object

Subject + Verb	Preposition	Prepositional Object
The match depends	on	rain.
He called	on	the Principal.
She depends	on	her parents.
He succeeded in	in	getting an employment.
Look	at	the red sky.
He believes	in	attacking with words.
I should not think	of	playing such a dirty game.
I rely	on	my conscience.
I will arrange	for	money.
They will arrange	for	a hall for the meeting.

Number of sentences 10

31. Subject + Verb + to + Infinitive

Subject + Veacrb	to + Infinitive
We stopped	to have meal.
I am waiting	to hear your decision.
I have come	To finish the job.

Number of sentences 3

32. Subject + Verb + to + Infinitive

Subject + Verb	to + Infinitive
How did he live	to be ninety?
How do you come	to know the accident?
How can I get	to know her address?

Number of sentences 3

33. Subject + Verb + to + Infinitive

Subject + Verb	to + Infinitive
He awake	to find the factory at fire.
The old man has gone not	to return.
She trembled	To hear it.

Number of sentences 3

34. Subject + Verb + to + Infinitive

Subject + Verb	to + Infinitive
I chanced	to notice them in a hotel.
Do you happen	to know where she is?
They seemed	not to notice the incident.

Number of sentences 3

35. Subject + Verb + to + Infinitive

Subject + Verb	to + Infinitive
They are	to be married soon.
Nobody is	to know the reason.
This I was only	to learn later.

Number of sentences 3

Chapter-8

Idioms

Idioms may be defined as expressions peculiar to a language. They play an important part in all languages. An idiom is basically a phrase where the words together have a meaning that is different from the dictionary definitions of the individual words.

May verbs, when followed by various prepositions or adverbs acquire an idiomatic sense; as,

He backed up (supported) his friend's claim.

Rust has eaten away (corroded) the plate.

Please hear me out (i.e., hear me to the end).

I have hit upon (found) a good plan to get rid of him.

About an hour ago I saw a fellow hanging about (loitering about) our bungalow.

BEAR
Satish bore away many prizes at the school sports. (Won)

A religious hope bears up (supports) a man in his trials.

BREAK
He broke down (failed) in the middle of his speech.

I gave him no cause to break with (quarrel with) me.

BRING
His folly ahs brought about (caused) his ruin.

He found great difficulty in bringing her round (converting her) to his views.

CALL
His master called for (demanded) an explanation of his conduct.

Call in (summon, send for) a doctor immediately.

CARRY
He agreed to carry out (execute) my orders.

His passion carried him away (i.e., deprived him of self-control).

CAST
The ship was cast away (wrecked) on the coast of Africa.

He was much cast down (depressed) by his loss.

COME
How did these things come about (happen)?

How did you come by (get) his purse?

CRY
He cried out against (protested against) such injustice.

That young author is cried up (extolled) by his friends.

CUT
He was cut off (died) in the prime of life3.

You must cut down (reduce) you expenditure.

DO
I am done for (ruined).

Having walked twenty miles, he is quite done up (fatigued, exhausted).

FALL
At last the rioters fell back. (Retreated, yielded).

At my friend's tea-party I fell with (met accidentally) a strange fellow.

GET
His friends expected that he would get off (escape) with a fine.

It is hard to get on with (agree or live sociably with) a suspicious man.

GIVE
The doctor have given him up (I.e., have no hope of his recovery).

The fire gave off (emitted) a dense smoke.

GO
You cannot always go by (judge from) appearances.

It is a good rule to go by (to be guided by).

HOLD
The rebels held out (offered resistance) for about a month.

They were held up (stopped on the highway and robbed) by bandits.

KEEP
A few boys were kept in (confined after school hours).

I was kept in (confined to the house) by a bad cold.

KNOCK
He has knocked about (wandered about) the world a great deal.

The dressing –table was knocked down (sold at an auction) for fifty rupees.

LAY
The rebels laid sown (surrendered) their arms.

Foolish people, who do not lay out (spend) their money carefully, soon come to grief.

LET
I was let into (made acquainted with) her secret.

This being his first offence he was let off (punished leniently) with a fine.

LOOK
His uncle looks after (takes care of) him.

I will look into (investigate) the matter.

MAKE
Contentment makes for (conduct to) happiness.

I cannot make out (discover) the meaning of this verse.

PASS
He generally passed by (overlooked) the faults of his subordinates.

The crew of the boat passed through (underwent) terrible sufferings.

PULL
Unless we pull together (co-operate, work together in harmony) we cannot succeed.

It is far easier to pull down (demolish) than to build up.

PUT
He puts on (assumes) an air of dignity.

Please put out (extinguish) the light.

RUN
On account of over wok he is run down (enfeebled).

He always runs down (disparages) his rivals.

SET
He immediately set about (took steps towards) organizing the department.

He has set up (started business) as a banker.

STAND
They are determined to stand up for (vindicate, maintain) their rights.

Let this matter stand over (be deferred or postponed) for the present.

THROW
My advice was thrown away (wasted) upon him, because he ignored it.

The bill was thrown out (rejected) by the assembly.

WORK
He worked out (solved) the problem in a few minutes.

He worked upon (influenced) the ignorant villagers.

Hence, we can conclude that an Idiom is a combination of words that has a figurative meaning due to its common usage. An Idiom's figurative meaning is separate from the literal meaning or definition of the words of which it is made. Idioms are numerous and they occur frequently in all languages. There are about 25,000 idiomatic expression in the English language.

Exercises

A

1. Choose the correct meaning of the Idiom from the Four Options given in each case.

1. **To end in smoke**
   - ❏ Smoking too many cigarettes
   - ❏ Face failure
   - ❏ House burnt down
   - ❏ Religious ceremony

2. **To get into hot waters**
   - ❏ Bathe in the winter months
   - ❏ To get rich
   - ❏ To get healthy
   - ❏ To get into trouble

3. **To make ends meet**
   - ❏ A short story
   - ❏ To skip classes
   - ❏ To earn enough to live
   - ❏ To be an expert

4. **Bolt from the blue**
   - ❏ Sudden shock
   - ❏ To lose a tight game
   - ❏ To get punched
   - ❏ To ask for help

5. **To burn the candle at both ends**
   - ❏ To argue endlessly
   - ❏ To work long hours
   - ❏ Long power cut
   - ❏ To have a good time

6. **To bury the hatchet**
   - ❏ To end enmity
   - ❏ To hide stolen treasure
   - ❏ To kill someone
   - ❏ To overexert

7. **To spill the beans**
   - ❏ To eat clumsily
   - ❏ To get exhausted
   - ❏ To reveal a secret
   - ❏ To fight

8. **To lead someone up the garden path**
   - ❏ To give directions
   - ❏ To mislead someone
   - ❏ To show a beautiful place
   - ❏ To exaggerate

9. **To weather a storm**
   - ❑ To criticise someone
   - ❑ To be an introvert
   - ❑ To survive a crisis
   - ❑ To guess correctly
10. **To bite one's lip**
    - ❑ To be unsure
    - ❑ To not react despite being angry
    - ❑ To feel sorry at someone's plight
    - ❑ To laugh at someone's misfortune

2. Choose the correct meaning of the Idiom in each case from the given options.

1. **What does the idiom 'to foam at one's mouth' mean?**
   a) to get very angry
   b) To brush vigorously so that foam forms in your mouth.
   c) To salivate on seeing food

2. **To 'feel like a fish out of water' is to feel**
   a) unhappy
   b) uncomfortable
   c) angry
   d) dejected

3. **When something is done at the eleventh hour, it is done**
   a) too early
   b) too late
   c) immediately
   d) at the last minute

4. **What do you mean when you say you have burnt your fingers?**
   a) that you have suffered financial losses
   b) that you have got hurt physically
   c) that you have to find work
   d) that you have just had a miraculous escape

5. **What do you mean by the idiom 'add fuel to fire'?**
   a) to say or do something that would make a bad situation even worse
   b) to investigate something
   c) to initiate something
   d) none of these

6. **What does the idiom 'off the top of your head' mean?**
   a) to say something without thinking much
   b) to do something that would put you in trouble
   c) to act recklessly
   d) none of these

Idioms

Answers

A-1 (1) Face failure (2) To get into trouble (3) To earn enough to live (4) Sudden shock, (5) To work long hours (6) To end enmity (7) To reveal a secret (8) To mislead someone (9) To survive a crisis (10) To not react despite being angry.

A-2 (1) To get very angry (2) To feel uncomfortable (3) It is done too late (4) That you have suffered financial losses (5) to say or do something that would make a bad situation even worse (6) To say something without thinking much

Chapter-9

Phrases, Proverbs and Expressions

Phrases: These are *groups of words* acting as a *single part of speech* and do not contain both a *subject* and a *verb*. *It is basically a part of a sentence, and does not express a complete thought.* A Phrase is generally a group of words acting as a single unit in a sentence which makes some sense, but not the complete sense.

For Example: The house *at the end of this street* is mine.

At the end of this street: Phrase—It is an **Adjective Phrase** as it qualifies **the noun or the subject**, *The house*.

There is one more phrase within this phrase – *Of this street:* **Prepositional Phrase,** as it tells us the location of the place.

Proverbs: *These are commonly used sentences which are simple and express a common truth or practical knowledge. Proverbs are also called Sayings.*

For Example:
  1. It takes two to tango.(which indicates teamwork)
  2. Let bygones be bygones. (which implies to forget the past)
  3. Love sees no fault. (another variation of love is blind)
  4. Look before you leap. (to cross check your plans before converting them to actions)
  5. Mind you own business. (to not interfere in other's life/work)

So, basically proverbs and idioms come under the 'sayings category'. However, an Idiom's meaning can't be made out at the first sight if we don't know where it's being used, whereas, a proverb is a practical thought or words of wisdom, in short.

Expressions: Expressions are generally a phrase where the words together have a meaning, that is different from the dictionary definitions of the individual words. There are around **3,819 idiomatic expressions with definitions** available in English Grammar.

Examples: (The meanings of these Idiomatic Expressions have been given below.)
- A penny for your thoughts
- Add insult to injury
- A hot potato
- Once in a blue moon
- Caught between two stools
- See eye to eye
- Hear it on the grapevine

- ❑ Miss the boat
- ❑ Kill two birds with one stone
- ❑ On the ball

Meanings:
- ❑ Cut corners
- ❑ To hear something straight from the horse's mouth
- ❑ Costs an arm and a leg
- ❑ The last straw
- ❑ Take what someone says with a pinch of salt
- ❑ Sit on the fence
- ❑ The best of both worlds
- ❑ Put wool over other people's eyes
- ❑ Feeling a bit under the weather
- ❑ Speak of the devil!

Following are some more examples of Phrases, Proverbs and Idiomatic Expressions:

1.
- ❑ In spite of all his bragging he <u>had to eat humble pie</u>.
- ❑ Take care what you say! You will have to <u>eat your words</u>.
- ❑ It is silly <u>to meet trouble half-way</u>.
- ❑ This is <u>of a piece</u> with the rest of his conduct.
- ❑ He is not <u>worth his salt</u> if he fails at this juncture.

2.
- ❑ The belief in witchcraft is <u>losing ground</u>.
- ❑ It was in parliamentary debate that he <u>won his spurs</u>.
- ❑ How can you trust a man who <u>plays fast and loose</u>.
- ❑ I <u>took him to task</u> for reading 'penny dreadfuls'.
- ❑ He <u>turned a deaf ear</u> to my advice.

3.
- ❑ The singer having a slight cough <u>was not in voice</u> at the concert.
- ❑ At least on the question of child-marriage, <u>we are at one</u>.
- ❑ He took my advice <u>in good part</u>.
- ❑ Steady work is sure to be rewarded <u>in the long run</u>.
- ❑ She <u>stood by him through thick and thin</u>.

4.
- He turns even his <u>errors to account</u>.
- He is accused of <u>sitting on the fence</u>.
- It is <u>all one to me</u> whether he lives in Mumbai or Kolkata.
- He spent over it much time and energy and lost a large sum <u>in the bargain</u>.
- Recently, he has been <u>giving himself airs</u>.

5.
- Poor fellow! He is <u>hoping against hope</u>.
- I am told he has <u>got the better of him</u>.
- The situation seems to have got quite <u>out of hand</u>.
- It is said that he has <u>finger in the pie</u>.
- That fellow <u>sets everybody by the ears</u>.

Exercises

Identify and Underline the Phrases/Proverbs in the following sentences.

1.
- Today he is in high spirits.
- Prohibition is gall and wormwood to distillers.
- The screen is in character with the rest of the furniture.
- I am afraid I am in his bad books.
- The thief took to his heels on seeing a policeman

2.
- He keeps in touch with the latest developments in wireless.
- The scheme appears worthless at the first blush.
- I smell a rat.
- He changed colour when I questioned him about his antecedents.
- I took him to task for his carelessness.

3.
- Naturally he fights shy of his young nephew, who is a gambler.
- The old man is hard of hearing.
- I trusted him and he played me false.
- I am out of pocket by the transaction.
- He is working against time.

4.
- I am afraid he is burning the candles at both ends.
- Late in life he tried his hand at farming.
- Throughout his speech the boys were all ears.
- While he was speaking his father cut him short.
- Stick to your colours, my boys!

5.
- A dispute in a south Wales colliery came to a head.
- He is rather blunt, but his heart is in the right place.

- I did not notice in him anything out of the way.
- In the contest he came off second-best.
- The usurper cannot maintain his position without the sinews of war.

Chapter-10

Miscellaneous Exercises

1. **Write the sentences and frame at least two sentences of your own following the pattern of each sentence.**

		the large red ball.
He	took out	the long yellow.
She	put down	the small green book.
Sweta	picked up	a white cricket ball.
Seema	rubbed with	a sharp knife.
Shashi	threw away	a steel pan.

Note: The maximum number of sentences you can form will be 150 + 300

2. **Write the sentences and frame at least two sentences of your own following the pattern of each sentence.**

They worked	all the day.
They played	throughout the morning.
They worshipped God	during the evening.
They sang hymns	from two o'clock.
They performed sacrifices	from six o'clock till noon.
He meditated	for two hours.
He practised yoga	from ten thirty sharp.
She looked after the guests	for many days.
They learnt lessons	until two o'clock.
The manager searched the file	till the evening.
The lady remained engaged	From eleven AM to 3 PM.

3. **Subject + Verb + Noun/ Pronoun + to/ not to + Infinite, etc.**

Subject + Verb	Noun/ Pronoun	to/ not to + Infinite etc
He wants	Me	to be early.
I asked	him	not to do it.
I told	the servant	to open the window.
Please help	me	to carry this box.
He likes	his wife	to dress well.

Your teachers expects	you	to work hard.
I warned	him	not to be late.
He allowed	the soldiers	to take him prisoner.
They have never known	him	to behave so well.

Note: The maximum number of sentences = 9 + 45 + 9=63

Also make the passive form also *i.e., He was warned not to be late.*

4. Subject + Verb + Noun/ Pronoun + (to be) + Complement

Subject + Verb	Noun/ Pronoun	(to be)	Complement
They believed	Him	(to be will be used in passive only)	innocent.
Do you consider	her		laborious?
I feel	it		unhealthy.
His mother	him		a clever boy.
We proved	him		wrong.

Note: The maximum number of sentences that you can get = 5 + 5 = 10

Also make the passive form:
He was believed innocent.
He was believed to be innocent.
Is she considered laborious?
Is she considered to be laborious?

5. Subject + Verb + Noun/ Pronoun + Infinitive, etc.

Subject + Verb	Noun/ Pronoun	Infinitive etc
She will have	him	do the work.
She heard	him	go out.
We saw	them	come in.
They felt	the bus	moving.
Watch	me	do it.
Did you notice	the thief	leave the house.
She made	him	work hard.
Let	them	go.
Don't let	the matter	aggravate.
They will help	me	carry this load.
Would you have	me	believe that?
We have never known	him	behave so badly.

Note: The maximum number of sentences you can form= 12 + 12=24

Miscellaneous Exercises

Also make the Passive Form:

He was made to work hard.

The bus was felt moving.

6. Subject + Verb + Noun/ Pronoun + Present Participle

Subject + Verb	Noun/ Pronoun	Present Participle
We watched	the train	leaving the station.
Do you feel	the house	shaking?
Can you smell	something	burning?
I saw	him	tumbling down.
He kept	me	waiting.
I found	him	working late.
They left	me	alone.
I heard	her	weeping.

Note: The maximum number of sentences that you can get=8 + 8

Make the Passive Form:

I was kept waiting.

She was heard weeping.

7. Subject + Verb + Object + Adjective

Subject + Verb	Object	Adjective
Do not get	your books	torn.
The moon keeps	the nights	cool.
Don't make	yourself	lazy.
Get	the room	furnished.
I found	the box	missing.
He painted	the gate	blue.
They set	the bird	free.
Please push	the door	open.
Winter turned	the leaves	yellow.
The doctor found	the patient	dead.

Note: The maximum number of sentences = 10 + 10=20

Change them into Passive Voice:

The box was found missing.

The gate was painted blue.

The bird was set free.

8. Subject + Verb + Object + Noun

Subject + Verb	Object	Noun
We elected	him	president.
The team crowned	him	captain.
The board chose	Mr. Gupta	Managing Director.
He named	the house	'Heaven'.
The parents call	their son	Umang.
The win made	the captain	hero.
The management declared	her	Principal.
They made	the clerk	manager.

Note: The maximum number of sentences that you will get = 8 + 8 =16

Change into Passive Voice:
The house was named 'Heaven'.
She was declared principal.

9. Subject + Verb + Object + Past Participle

Subject + Verb	Object	Past Participle
She must get	her hair	cleaned.
Where did you get	them	posted?
Has she	a new car	bought?
Have you ever heard	Samskrit	recited?
His book has	a reward	Fetched.
The police had	a criminal	encountered.
Why did you get	them	printed?
Has he	his new book	Given?

Number of sentences = 8

10. Subject + Verb + Object + Adverb/ Adverbial Phrase

Subject + Verb	Object	Adverb/ Adverbial Phrase
They treat	the girl	as if a maid.
He takes	a day	off.
Put	the book	here.
I don't know	him	to speak to.
They led	me	to feel safe.
They invited	the groom	to meet the bride.
He went to	the clinic	as advised by the doctor.

Miscellaneous Exercises

She performed	a solo	to raise money.
He has given	it	away.
They brought	the girl	to see me.
He showed	me	to the car.

Number of sentences = 11

11. Subject + Verb + Noun/ Pronoun + (that) Clause

Subject + Verb	(that) Clause
I hope	(that) you will come.
I suppose	(that) you will be there.
He explained	(that) nothing could be done.
Do you think	(that) it will rain?
He saw	(that) the plan was useless.
I suggest	(that) he should leave early.

Number of sentences = 6 + 6

Change into Passive on the pattern given below:

It was explained that nothing could be done.

It was seen that the plan was useless.

12. Subject + Verb + Noun/ Pronoun + (that) Clause

Subject + Verb	Noun/ Pronoun	(that) Clause
I told	the man	(that)
I warned	you	(that)
We satisfied	ourselves	(that)
Please remind	him	(that)

Number of sentences = 4

13. Subject + Verb + Conjunctive + to Infinitive

Subject + Verb	Conjunctive	to Infinitive
I wonder	how	To do it.
I do not know	what	to do.
He is learning	how	to swim.
She was wondering	which	to buy.
Will you find out	how	to get there.
You must remember	when	to begin.
I do not know	whether	to go or stay.

Number of sentences = 7

14. Subject + Verb + Noun/ Pronoun + Conjunctive + to Infinitive

Subject + Verb	Noun/ Pronoun	Conjunctive	to Infinitive
We showed	him	how	to do it.
Please tell	me	which	to take.
Can you advise	me	which	to buy?
The patterns show	you	how	to make sentences.
Tell	me	whether	to come or not.
They told	him	when	to start.
Tell	her	what	to do.

Number of sentences = 7 + 7

Change into Passive Voice on the pattern given below:

He was showed how to do it.

He was told when to start.

15. Subject + Verb + Conjunctive + Clause

Subject + Verb	Conjunctive	Clause
I wonder	why	he has not come.
I wonder	whether / if	he will come.
I do not mind	where	we go.
Do you know	who	he is?
I do not care	what	you think.
Can you suggest	where	this ought to go?
Please say	what	you want.
Nobody says	whose	It is.

Number of sentences = 8

16. Subject + Verb

Subject + Verb	Noun/ Pronoun	Conjunctive	Clause
Tell	me	what	it is.
Ask	him	where	he put it.
They asked	us	when	we should be back.
Can you tell	me	how	high it is?
Can you inform	me	when	the train leaves.
Please advise	me	when	these seeds should be sown.

Number of sentences = 6

Miscellaneous Exercises

17. Subject + Verb + Gerund

Subject + Verb	Gerund
Please stop	talking.
He enjoys	playing tennis.
I remember	doing it.
Please excuse	me being so late.
Do you mind	staying a little longer?
Do you mind	my staying a little longer?
She could not	laughing.
He keeps on	coming here.
They went on	talking.
Has it left off	raining yet.

Number of sentences = 10

18. Subject + Verb + Gerund etc.

Combine each of the first part with each of the second part to frame separate sentences.

Subject + Verb	Gerund etc
He began	talking./ to talk.
He likes	swimming./ to swim.
I prefer	staying indoors./ to stay indoors.
I hate	refusing every time./ to refuse every time.
He started	packing books./ to pack his books.

Number of sentences = 25 + 25

19. Subject + Verb + Gerund, etc.

Combine each of the first part with each of the second part, to frame separate Sentences.

Subject + Verb	Gerund etc (Passive Infinite)
It wants	elaborating. / to be elaborated.
Your work needs	correcting. / to be corrected.
That needs	explaining. / to be explained.
He needs	refreshing. / to be refreshed.

Number of sentences = 16 + 16 = 32

20. Subject + Verb + Direct Object + Preposition + Prepositional Object

Subject + Verb		Preposition	
I gave	the money	to	my friend.
They told	the news	to	everybody they met.
We showed	the pictures	to	our teachers.
I do not lend	my books	to	anybody.
He offered	once	to	me.
I owe	thirty rupees	to	my tailor.
Throw	that box	to	me.
Bring	that book	to	me.

Number of sentences = 8

21. Subject + Verb+ Direct Object + Preposition + Prepositional Object

Subject + Verb	Direct Object	Preposition	Prepositional object
He bought	a necklace	for	the bride.
He gifted	a gold watch	to	his wife.
Please give	some	for	me.
They left	a message	for	the commander.
She made	a new dress	for	herself.
Have you left	any	for	your sister.
Please get	two tickets	for	me.
They selected	a bride	for	their son.

Number of sentences = 8

22. Subject + Verb+ Direct Object + Preposition + Prepositional Object

Subject + Verb	Direct Object	Preposition	Prepositional Object
Thank	you	for	your kind help.
Ask	him	for	a few more.
Compare	this	with	that flag.
They punished	him	for	being very late.
Congratulate	him	on	his grand success.
Do not throw	the stone	at	the poor donkey.
What prevented	you	from	joining the post?
Add	this	to	what you have.
I explained	my difficulty	to	the manager.
Protect	us	from	the terrorists.

Number of sentences = 10

Miscellaneous Exercises

23. Subject + Verb + Indirect Object + Direct Object

Subject + Verb	Indirect Object	Direct Object
Have they paid	you	the subscription?
Will you lend	me	your book?
Did our teacher give	us	home work?
Did I read	him	the newspaper?
Please throw	me	a pen.
His grand father told	him	a nice story.
He handed	me	the cheque.
The pupils wished	the teachers	'Happy New Year.'
He denies	her	nothing essential.

Number of sentences = 9

24. Subject + Verb + Indirect Object + Direct Object

Subject + Verb	Indirect Object	Direct Object
She made	herself	a nice bag.
Her father bought	me	a new dress.
Please buy	me	a cup of tea.
Did you leave	her	a message?
She ordered	him	a pass.
Will you do	her	a favour?
Can you spare	me	a bed for the night?
Can you get	me	a ticket for me?

Number of sentences = 8

25. Subject + Verb + Direct Object I + Direct Object II

Subject + Verb	Direct Object I	Direct Object II
Forgive	him	his childish behaviour.
They asked	me	the secret.
They smeared	me	ink.
They saved	me	a great deal of trouble.
I envy	you	for the fine house.
Forgive	us	our mistakes.
That will save	me	some money.
I struck	him	a heavy blow.
I gave	him	an upper cut.
He asked	me	a question.

Number of sentences = 10

26. Subject + Verb + (for) Complement

Subject + Verb	(for) Complement
We walked	(for) five kilometers.
They had come	a long way.
The forest stretched	(for) miles and miles.
The rain lasted	all day long.
He may live	(for) many more years.
They waited	(for) four hours.
The temperature rose	five degrees.
It weighs	eighty kilograms.
It costs	One thousand.
Will she stay	(for) the night?

Number of sentences = 13

27. Subject + Verb

Subject	Verb
Fire	burns.
Birds	flew.
We all	eat, drink, breathe and sleep.
The moon	shines.
The sun	rose.
A cat	jumped.
Bees	fly.
Boys	play.
A child	cried.
A writer	writes.

Number of sentences = 10

28. Subject + Verb

Predicative is that part of a general sentence that follows the verb and gives information about the subject of the sentence. It (the Predicative) may be an Adjective, Adjective Phrase, Noun or Pronoun.

Subject + Verb	Predicative
This is	a table.
This box	is yours.
That will be	enough.
Please get	to receive her.

Miscellaneous Exercises

The weather has become	colder.
The leaves have turned	yellow.
It feels	smooth and cold.
The plan proved	a boon.
The results are	quite unexpected.
His dream came	true.
The curd turned	sour.

Number of sentences = 11

Note: *This Verb Pattern is used in various ways with slight variations. The following are some variants of this Verb Pattern. Frame at least five sentences on each of these patterns.*

With Preparatory it: e.g.
- ❏ It is easy to say so.
- ❏ It is a pity he could not pass.
- ❏ It is no use your trying to mend it.
- ❏ It would be sad to waste it.

With an Infinitive Phrase as complement: e.g.
- ❏ This shop is to let.
- ❏ To see her is to appreciate her.
- ❏ My aim is to encourage the students.

With the subject complement first: e.g.
- ❏ What is that?
- ❏ What are you holding?
- ❏ What price is that suit?

With an Adverb or Prepositional Phrase as the complement: e.g.
- ❏ She is in good mood.
- ❏ The car is out of order.
- ❏ The boy is out of control.
- ❏ The fruit is far too ripe.

29. Subject + Verb

Subject + Verb	Adverbial Adjunct
Stand	up!
Sit	down!
Turn	back!
The sun sets	in the west.
We did not go	anywhere.
He will go	as soon as he is ready.

| I will help | as much as practicable. |
| A piece of furniture will not stand | on two legs. |

Number of sentences = 8

30. Subject + Verb + Preposition + Prepositional Object

Subject + Verb	Preposition	Prepositional Object
The match depends	on	rain.
He called	on	the Principal.
She depends	on	her parents.
He succeeded in	in	getting an employment.
Look	at	the red sky.
He believes	in	attacking with words.
I should not think	of	playing such a dirty game.
I rely	on	my conscience.
I will arrange	for	money.
They will arrange	for	a hall for the meeting.

Number of sentences = 10

31. Subject + Verb + to + Infinitive

Subject + Verb	to + Infinitive
We stopped	to have meal.
I am waiting	to hear your decision.
I have come	To finish the job.

Number of sentences = 3

32. Subject + Verb + to + Infinitive

Subject + Verb	to + Infinitive
How did he live	to be ninety?
How do you come	to know the accident?
How can I get	to know her address?

Number of sentences = 3

33. Subject + Verb + to + Infinitive

Subject + Verb	to + Infinitive
He awoke	to find the factory at fire.
The old man has gone not	to return.
She trembled	To hear it.

Number of sentences = 3

34. Subject + Verb + to + Infinitive

Subject + Verb	to + Infinitive
I chanced	to notice them in a hotel.
Do you happen	to know where she is?
They seemed	not to notice the incident.

Number of sentences = 3

35. Subject + Verb + to + Infinitive

Subject + Verb	to + Infinitive
They are	to be married soon.
Nobody is	to know the reason.
This I was only	to learn later.

Number of sentences = 3

Exercises

Exercise 1

Write the sentences and frame at least two sentences of your own following the pattern of each Sentence.

		the large red ball.
He	took out	the long yellow.
She	put down	the small green book.
Sweta	picked up	a white cricket ball.
Seema	rubbed with	a sharp knife.
Shashi	threw away	a steel pan.

Number of sentences = 150 + 300

Exercise 2

Write the sentences and frame at least two sentences of your own following the pattern of each sentence.

They worked	all the day.
They played	throughout the morning.
They worshipped God	during the evening.
They sang hymns	from two o'clock.
They performed sacrifices	from six o'clock till noon.
He meditated	for two hours.
He practised yoga	from ten thirty sharp.
She looked after the guests	for many days.
They learnt lessons	until two o'clock.
The manager searched the file	till the evening.
The lady remained engaged	From eleven AM to 3 PM.

Number of sentences = 121 + 242

Miscellaneous Exercises

Exercise 3

Write the sentences and frame at least two sentences of your own following the pattern of each sentence.

The sun always rises	
The sun never sets	in the east.
The sun shines	during the day.
The students go to school	during the morning hours.
Everything shines	with a hope.
A lot of knowledge comes first	faithfully.
All the light is scattered first	

Number of sentences = 35 + 70

Exercise 4

Write the Sentences and frame at least two Sentences of your own following the pattern of each Sentence.

I write Aum, the symbol of Brahma	
We eat something	every Thursday.
We visit the temple	every morning.
We have lessons	once everyday.
They clean the shop	thrice daily.
He works at a hall and goes there	without fail.
We play the tabala	regularly.
We take lessons in music	

Number of sentences = 48 + 96

Exercise 5

Write the sentences and frame at least two sentences of your own following the pattern of each sentence.

		been to Varanasi.
He has	once	been up in an airplane.
There are people that have	often	seen women fighting.
All philanthropic persons have	twice	found courageous faring well.
These worshippers have	never	helped the poor and needy.
		been selected in the preliminary.
		encountered true devotees.

Number of sentences = 112 + 224

Exercise 6

Write the sentences and frame at least two sentences of your own following the pattern of each sentence.

There are still some green trees	
There must be fruit trees	in all regions.
We must plant and protect trees	along the sides of the roads.
They have deputed volunteers	in each garden and field.
They are arranging free feasts	At vacant places
They drew some demarcating lines	
There are heaps of garbage	

Number of sentences = 28 + 56

Exercise 7

Write the sentences and frame at least two sentences of your own following the pattern of each sentence.

Shekhar spends a lot	on books.
Mr Sinha spends a lot of time	on study.
She spends very little money	on tuition.
Mr. Thakur spends nothing	on healthy growth.
I have been regularly spending something	on junk food.
Everyone must spend	on fresh vegetables.

Number of sentences = 36 + 72

Exercise 8

Write (a) answers to the questions; and (b) change them into affirmative sentences.

Is the man with white cap sitting or standing?
What is the man with an iron ladder doing?
Why is the sound of the machine is not coming?
Why is the printer taking many pages at a time?
What colour is the shirt that I gave you yesterday?
Where did you keep the attendance register?
Where can I get a few boxes of white chalk?
Why did she give you a hard pencil?
Where did you buy that green book with yellow pages?
How can the long holidays be happily spent?

Number of sentences = 10 + 20

Exercise 9

Write the sentences and frame at least two sentences of your own following the pattern of each sentence.

I have not finished the drawing yet.
I'm still drawing the body.
I have already drawn the eyes.
She has placed many flowers in the vessel.
Some of the flowers are yellow and some are white.
Now, there are enough flowers in the pot.
Yet, some more flowers can be added to it.
The pot is too full to hold any more.
She poured water into the pot but not much.
A little work and the pot has increased the beauty many times.

Number of sentences 10 + 20

Exercise 10

Write the sentences and frame at least two sentences of your own following the pattern of each sentence.

She hit herself with the roller.
While cutting vegetables you yourself have injured your fingers.
I must blame myself for coming late.
One must feel the burden of responsibility on oneself.
We have tried hard to start the machine ourselves.
He himself dug his grave by allowing aliens to live with him.
They themselves assembled the complete computer set.
The plate itself slipped down from the rack.

Number of sentences 8 + 16

Exercise 11

I. Frame at least one sentence with each weak and strong verb.
II. Read, understand, learn and imbibe all the weak and strong verbs and keep them on the tip of tongue and pen. One can't learn English without having command of V1, V2 and V3.
III. Read a book on English Grammar from page one to the last and solve all the exercises given in it. The reading of the total book without leaving anything out will give you a complete picture of English language. Never think of important and unimportant chapters. Everything and all the chapters are important. If they are not important then they would not have been there.

IV. Remember to write a complete sentence every time. Don't write one part many times then the other part that many time to show to the teacher of guardian that you have completed the task. It is not solving task, it is learning.
V. Complete sentences will give 'completeness' to your knowledge and ability.
VI. Writing many pages a day will bear fruits in their own way, according to their capacity but they are bound to teach you. Remember: Reading makes a wise man; speaking makes a ready man but writing makes a perfect man.
VII. Frame sentences of your own: as many as you can within the available time limit. It will give command over spelling and punctuation. This practice from an early age will bear immense sweet fruits later on during maturity when all the sentence pattern are a part and parcel of consciousness.
VIII. Always keep a handy Dictionary at hand. Collect and obtain mastery over the words. Remember: there are neither easy words nor difficult words; words are either known or unknown; and they help.
IX. Remember your God; have patience, courage and confidence; and go ahead. You are the winner.

Prepositions, Clauses and Others

1. Prepositions

		apple tree						
		ox						
An		owl	is		in		the	field.
		onion carton	was		around			garden.
		orange-box						hut.
		elephant						house.
		old woman						
		oil-can						

Number of sentences = 128

2. Prepositions

An officer	came	to me.
An official messenger	came fast	to her house.
An agent	was coming	from the southern end.
An old car	was not coming	with some papers.
An air courier	did not come	on an urgent mission.
An applicant	will come	for consultation.
	will not come	Without an appointment.

Number of sentences = 294

Miscellaneous Exercises

3. Prepositions

The book		on the table.
The pen		in the bag.
The pencil	is	in the box.
The copy	was	in the drawer.
The diary	will be	at the top of the almirah.
The register	is not	behind the rack.
The key	was not	by the books.
The file	will not be	under the table
The pictures		under the chair.
The watch		beside the mirror.

Number of sentences = 600

4. Prepositions

The book			on the table.
The pen			in the bag.
The pencil	is	kept	in the box.
The copy	was	lying	in the drawer.
The diary	will be		at the top of the almirah.
The register	is not		behind the rack.
The key	was not		by the books.
The file	will not be		under the table
The pictures			under the chair.
The watch			beside the mirror.

Number of sentences = 1200

5. Prepositions

They		in	India.
The technicians	fought	for	the University.
The employees	called a strike	out of	the factory.
The people	created a scene	against	

Number of sentences = 194

6. Prepositions

The book		above my head.
The pen		above my shoulder.
The pencil	has been	by the wall.
The copy	had been	by the rack.
The diary	has been lying	without cover.
The register	had been lying	out of sight.
The key	has not been lying	out of my reach.
The file	had not been lying	before me.
The pictures		behind the librarian.
The watch		on the shelf.

Number of sentences = 600

7. Prepositions

He		waiting for a bus.
She		planning to go on a picnic.
Rajesh	is	working for many years.
Zafar	was	earning a lot of money.
My mother	has been	walking without a stick.
Her sister	had been	roaming on foot.
Your uncle	will be	running with an aim.
The manager		speaking in a meeting.

Number of sentences = 284

8. Prepositions

		working with a motive.
		writing for a magazine.
We	are	looking for a job.
They	were	running around.
You	have been	moving from pillar to post.
	had been	switching off the lights.
	will be	pulling it up.
	will not be	throwing that down.
		relaxing on the sofa.
		lying by the wall.
		waiting at the ticket window.

Miscellaneous Exercises

| | | arriving in time. |
| | | present in the meeting. |

Number of sentences = 234

9. Prepositions

I have		for two months.
You have	lived here	for several years.
He has	worked there	for a long time.
She has	studied Grammar	for three years.
My friend has	been a lecturer	since 2005.
They have	practised as a doctor	since June last.
		since last Diwali.

Number of sentences = 210

10. Prepositions

All the		are walking	to the pond.
Both the	boys	walked	to the swimming pool.
Some of the	girls	will walk	to the market.
The other	persons	are going	to the book fair.
Some	students	went	away from the exhibition.
Five		will go	across the field.

Number of sentences = 576

11. Prepositions

He earns his living by	working in the factory.
He can establish peace by	strengthening union.
Mohan is fond of	learning languages.
Priya is clever at	teaching in a school.
Gita is interested in	singing religious songs.
Deepa has strong plea for	performing dances.
He became rich after	getting a good job.
He got money without	maintaining communal harmony.
You can do nothing without	

Number of sentences = 72

12. Prepositions

Sita,		these pens	
Ramesh,		this box	in your desk.
Rajesh,	please, put	that book	on my table.
Lipika,		these shirts	near the window.
Tanu,		the album	behind the door.
		the painting	

Number of sentences = 120

13. Prepositions

The nail			the table.
The hammer		in front of	the wardrobe.
The axe	is	behind	the show case.
The knife	was	in the middle of	the rack.
The nail-file		at the top of	the rack.
The rod		at the bottom of	the board.
The duster			the pot.
The medicine			the box.

Number of sentences = 768

14. Prepositions

There is a nice picture	in the hall.
There is a big desk	by the wall.
There is a small table	on the floor.
There are three black boxes	at the door.
There are four new chairs	in the truck.
There are five long benches	between the table.

15.

I	always	look at the pictures.
You	seldom	look through the window.
They	often	look down upon the misers.
The boys	usually	go home early.
		complete works in time.
		get up early.
		play football.

Miscellaneous Exercises

| | | read stories. |
| | | prepare the lessons. |

16.

'An apple for an apple'	
'An eye for an eye'	is the dictum.
'All is well that ends well'	is true for all time.
'He that leaps will fall'	is a famous proverb.
'Better late than never'	is the saying of wise men.
'Charity begins at home'	

Number of sentences = 24

17. Clauses

	what I am going to tell you.
	all that I have to say.
Plan carefully	the things that must be known.
Listen to	the future plan.
Listen carefully	the actions of future.
Listen and follow	the blue print of the work chart.
Remember	what you have to do.
	what is needed now.
	what is important.
	what was discussed in the meeting.

Number of sentences = 24

18. Clauses

				they have done.
I	can't			they have told.
You	can	justify	what	they have achieved.
He	must	understand	that which	they have overlooked.
	must not	remind	the thing that	they have forgotten.
	should			they have borrowed.
	should not			they are overlooking.
				is important.

Number of sentences = 756

19. Clauses

He will do that	if you want.
I shall speak to him	if you ask.
You will be informed	if it is requested.
He will accept the post	if a letter is given.
They would help you	if it is offered.
He would do it	if it is proved right.
I shall oppose him	if the deadlock continues.

Number of sentences = 49

20.

		bite.
I	continued to	come.
You	began to	speak.
They	used to	strike hard.
He		look down upon.
She		spend a lot.
People		read everything.
Boys		play only football.
		make a car.
		sing well.
		swim for a long time.
		shed tears.
		tell lies.
		throw away the money.

Number of sentences = 252

21.

I		breaking wood.
We	went on	going ahead.
You	kept on	singing songs.
He	started	reciting rhymes.
She		drinking cold water.
They		giving instructions.
People		telling a story.
Boys		reading poems.
Girls		running fast.

Number of sentences = 243

Miscellaneous Exercises

22.

I	informed		the banker will call at your place.
He	intimated	that	Sita was called for an explanation.
She	told the news		the doctor was called in time.
We	gave the information		the strike was called off.
They			the culprit was brought to book.
			they brought about their own ruin.

Number of sentences = 144

23.

Praveen	Called the doctor in.
They	Threw the ball away.
We	Cut the ribbon off.
I	Sent them back.
You	Put the gown on.
He	Called the strike off.
She	Put off the lamp.
Seema	Gave away the prizes.
The President	Was hit for three consecutive sixes.
His uncle	Foolishly played with flames.
Her brother	Looked into the matter.
My sister	Will abide by the rules.
	Will take care of the expenses.
	Will not stop in the middle.
	Will freely work for the children.

Number of sentences = 180

24. Comparisons

		pen			
This		book		charming	as that.
		watch	is as	beautiful	
		horse	is not as	pretty	
		house	is not so	useful	
		car		useless	

204   English Grammar And Usage

		curtain		dirty	
		office		pleasant	
		drawer		refreshing	
		incense			
		perfume			

Number of sentences = 264

25. Comparisons

	pen			
This	book	is more	charming	as that.
	watch	is less	beautiful	
	horse		pretty	
	house		useful	
	car		useless	
	curtain		dirty	
	office		pleasant	
	drawer		refreshing	
	incense			
	perfume			

Number of sentences = 176

26. Comparisons

	pen book watch horse house car curtain office drawer incense perfume	is the most is the least	charming beautiful pretty useful useless dirty pleasant refreshing	of all.
This				

Number of sentences = 176

Miscellaneous Exercises

27. Comparisons

This young man This boy This rich man This merchant This river This leader This manager	is as is not as is not so	idle truthful wicked popular greedy famous dangerous	as that.

Number of sentences = 147

28. Comparisons

This young man This boy This rich man This merchant This river This leader This manager	is more is less	idle truthful wicked popular greedy famous dangerous	as that.

Number of sentences = 147

29. Comparisons

This young man This boy This rich man This merchant This river This leader This manager	is the most is the least	idle truthful wicked popular greedy famous dangerous	as that.

Number of sentences = 147

30. Comparisons

| This leader
This pleader
This teacher
This young man
This boy
This rich man
This merchant
This river
This leader
This manager | is
was
will be | greater
wiser
cleverer
truer
more popular
more learned
more honest
more diligent | than that. |

Number of sentences = 240

31. Comparisons

| This leader
This pleader
This teacher
This young man
This boy
This rich man
This merchant
This river
This leader
This manager | is
was
will be | the greatest
the wisest
the most successful
the most worthy
more popular
more learned
more honest
more diligent | of all. |

Number of sentences = 240

Miscellaneous Exercises

32. Narration

		he is ill.
He says	that	he goes to school.
We know		he will go to school.
She fears		Mohan has done that.
You think		Mohan will do that.
He will say		the boy comes late.
I say		the boy would come late.
You hear		the birds are flying.
		the earth moves round the sun.
		an empty vessel sounds much.
		Ram killed Ravana.
		labour never goes in vain.
		honesty is the best policy.

Number of sentences = 91

33. Narration

		he would help.
He said		he would go there the next day.
I said		he has won the race.
You said	that	they were guilty.
We said		I was wrong.
They informed		he was tired.
The teacher said		she was very wicked.
Meera told		they were ready to help.
Seema was informed		the sun rises in the east.
They learnt		Ram was a student.
		Jaya was a scholar.

Number of Sentences 99

34.

I made		do it.
I forced	him	do the work.
We must not let	her	take rest here.
We saw	them	behave so badly.
I heard		carry the box.
We watched		return the loan.

Number of sentences = 108

35.

It is not necessary	for me to walk to the office.
There is no cause	for you to wait.
It is not too late	for the children to play.
It is difficult	for you to do this.
It is very easy	for anyone to control him.
It is not easy	for me to let him go.
	for me to the interest.
	for them to fight like this.

Number of sentences = 48

36.

We feel like	playing tennis.
We have started	helping others.
Don't give up	playing harmonium and flute.
I don't mind	dancing.
She likes	working in the garden.
I love	ding outdoor works.
Gopal prefers	painting portraits.
He prefers	taking notes.
Lata enjoys	solving spiritual problems.
They relish	showing compassion.

Number of sentences = 100

Miscellaneous Exercises

37.

I		working		he		drink.
They	kept on	moving	and	she	continued to	eat.
We		running		she		watch.
He		looking		Kamal		play.
She		serving		Kavita		run.
Raman		showing		the boys		read.
Sarita		writing		the girls		speak.

Number of sentences = 1658

38.

This is		cloth.
Please give		rod.
I want	a piece of	bamboo.
They bought	ten metres of	wire.
He donated		glass sheet.
		curtain.

Number of sentences = 60

39.

Please give me		tea.
I gave her		coffee.
He offered	a cup of	sugar.
I bought	a kilo of	ice-cream.
They are purchasing		fruit juice
		honey.

Number of sentences = 108

40.

He		sitting		Ram
She		running		Kishore
Ravi	is	waiting	next to	Mohan
Ramesh		moving		Dheeraj
Pankaj		walking		
Neeraj				

Number of sentences = 120

41.

I You They We	want like	to collect to buy to give to show	this picture. that pen. these bottles. those cards. ripe mangoes. magnetic chess. new Dictionaries.

Number of sentences = 256

42.

He She	likes wants	to collect to buy to give to show	this arrangement. that movie. these cartoon. fresh apples. ripe mangoes. magnet. new books

Number of sentences = 112

43.

I want to know Tell me I enquired I asked him I don't know	"What is your name?" Why are you angry?" "Where do you live?" "When will you finish the work?" "Why are you ill?" "Who will feed you?" "What have you eaten?" "When did you come here?"

Number of sentences = 40

44.

I want to know	what his name was.
Tell me	why he was angry.
I enquired	where he lives.
I asked him	when he would finish the work.
I don't know	why he was ill.
	who will feed him.
	what he had eaten.
	when he came there.

Number of sentences = 40

45.

He			innocent.
She		believed	honest.
The manager	is	considered	wise.
The clerk	was	proved	wrong.
		known	true.

	to be

Number of sentences = 160

46.

He			to open the window.
The servant			to be late.
The girl		told	to arrange the articles.
The tall man	was	called	to carry the boxes.
		forced	to clean the room.
		ordered	to participate in the function.
		asked	to collect the scattered books.
		allowed	to distribute the cards.

Number of sentences = 192

47.

He			waiting	
She		kept	working	by her son.
I	was	found	giving orders	for her.
		seen	leaving the station	by the boss.
		watched	standing outside	
			carrying boxes	
			cleaning the office	

Number of sentences = 360

212 English Grammar And Usage

48.

| The box
The door
The room
The locker
The drawer | was | found empty.
painted green.
dirty.
left open.
thoroughly cleaned. |

Number of sentences = 25

49.

| Had he been | told
warned
reminded
satisfied | that | he was mistaken
he would be late
he must come here early
nothing could be done
the plan was useless
he has a meeting | ? |

Number of sentences = 24

50.

| He was
We were
You were
Students were | shown
told
advised | how to do it.
when to start.
how to frame sentences.
which one to select.
what to take.
where to go.
what to leave behind. |

Number of sentences = 84

51.

| The man who was | running fast
driving a car
sitting behind me | asked me to run.
called me to say something.
was looking pale
was not known to me.
had gone mad.
will come again.
gave me his visiting card. |

Number of sentences = 84

Miscellaneous Exercises

52. Phrases

The negotiations will be finished	in a mysterious way.
I shall see you	before long.
He will get everything	without delay.
We will get a refusal	in black and white.
The plan will be discussed	right or wrong.
The situation will improve	in no time.

Number of sentences = 36

53.

The negotiations will be finished	in a mysterious way.
I shall see you	before long.
He will get everything	without delay.
We will get a refusal	in black and white.
The plan will be discussed	right or wrong.
The situation will improve obviously	in no time.

Number of sentences = 36

54.

	the face of	the clock.
	the front of	the water heater.
This is	the back of	the reservoir.
That is	the top of	the thermos.
	the bottom of	the swimming pool.

Number of sentences = 50

55.

These are		the maps.
Those are	the sides of	the charts.
		the black board.
		The box.

Number of sentences = 8

56.

| Everybody
Each one of us
He
Ravi | feels
seems
looks
appears to be | contented.
happy.
sad.
satisfied.
dissatisfied. |

Number of sentences = 80

57.

| He
She
Rita
Mohan
The boy
The girl | hardly
generally
some times
often
never
usually | comes here.
seeps well.
visits me.
comes to my place.
eats happily.
plays outside.
sings songs. |

Number of sentences = 84

58.

| The news
The result
The invitation | is
was | very interesting.
very surprising.
much admired.
conveyed in time.
published in advance.
shocking. |

Number of sentences = 36

59.

| I
We
They
My brothers
My friends | love
hate
prefer | lying on the back.
to lie on grass.
to rise up in early morning.
to work during afternoon.
sitting on hard chairs.
to sit on a cushioned sofa.
to burst out laughing.
to spend money.
to waste time. |

Number of sentences = 165

Miscellaneous Exercises

60.

| We He They | went there
did it
inaugurated it
finished the book
completed the work
raised the pillar
made a platform | yesterday.
last June.
two days ago.
last month. |

Number of sentences = 56

61.

| Each of them
Everyone
Neither of them
Either of them
One of the girls
Either he or she
Neither he nor she | is
was | rewarded.
present.
tall.
absent.
refined.
cultured.
diligent.
intelligent.
talented. |

Number of sentences = 126

62.

| The prisoner
The father
The teacher
The farmer
The inspector
The officer | is
was | angry with his son.
angry at what he had heard.
pleased with his performance.
interested in the story.
disillusioned about the future.
affected by the turn of events.
accused of partiality. |

Number of sentences = 84

63.
Add sign of Interrogation in the Interrogative sentences.

There's		ink in the bottle.
There is		Water in the river.
Is there	a lot of	Juice in the jug.
There isn't	much	Sugar in this bag.
There is not		Money in his wallet.
		Sand near the bank of the river.

Number of sentences = 60

64.

		match sticks in the match boxes.
There are	a few	books on the book shelf.
Are there	many	flowers in my garden.
There are not		flowering plants in my area.
		leaves on trees during winter.
		bags in the store.

Number of sentences = 36

65.

Please assist	him	to lift the suitcase.
She will help	her	to clean the cupboard.
I want	Shekhar	to bring down the iron stair.
Raman will go with		to adjust the freeze.

Number of sentences = 48

66. Phrases

He was beaten	in front of me.
He supported you	to get imaginary favour.
He was defeated	on account of ill-health.
He was victimised	in spite of hard labour.
He surrendered	owing to bad weather.
He left the job	against his will.

Number of sentences = 36

67.

		one.
Here is	another	pen.
There is		book.
I have seen		picture on page 51.
		map on the wall.
		beggar at the mosque.
		field of onion.
		set of tools.
		place for carpenters.
		mango orchard.

Number of sentences = 30

68.

Did you know			called?
Can they tell	what	this is	used for?
Did she explain		coal	made up of?
Can scientists analyse		glucose	

Number of sentences = 12+12 = 24

69.

I saw	the tallest tree.
They visited	the most beautiful city.
They live near	the highest mountain.
We are very close to	the oldest person.
We can't go to	the longest field.
	the largest stadium.
	the biggest market.

Number of sentences = 35

Exercise 1 - Compound Sentences

Match the sentences and frame at least two sentences of your own following the patterns of each synthesised sentence.

After burning the midnight oil	he topped in the class.
On hearing my voice	the child ran to me.
She has four children	to support.
I have much work	to do.
This is my student	Sunny.
Nehru, a famous writer	wrote the 'Discovery of India.'
Having finished this work	the workers left for home.
Being a true patriot	he will not betray his country.
In spite of being weak	he studies hard.
Frustrated with loss in business	he went mad.
While walking on the road	I saw a big dog.
Having finished his studies	he started his own agency.
Undoubtedly,	he is a great sportsman.
They had not arrived	till now.
You are taking up old issues	unnecessarily.

Number of sentences = 15 + 2 = 17

Exercise 2 - Compound Sentences

Match the sentences and frame at least two sentences of your own following the patterns of each Synthesised Sentence.

We went to the University	and studied there.
She is a coward	and a fool.
Kiran is both	intelligent and beautiful.
Neither a borrower	nor a lender be.
Either Rajan or Ravi	will have to face the situation.
Word hard	else you will fail.
Either pay the price	or return the pen.
I know Mohan	but not Ravi.
Though, I rebuked him	yet he kept mum.
Although, he lost his position	nevertheless, he kept his cool.
I don't believe in what you say	however, I shall not oppose you.
She stood first in the class	therefore, she was given a prize.
I can't depend on him	for he is a fool.
He is definitely	talented and diligent.

Number of sentences = 14 + 2 = 16

Miscellaneous Exercises

Exercise 3 - Complex Sentences

Match the sentences and frame at least two sentences of your own following the patterns of each Synthesised Sentence.

Everyone knows it	that he is an honest boy.
The fact that Bose was a great scientist	can not be challenged.
Ask him	why he is late.
I can not understand	what you say.
He is the boy	who stood first in his class.
This is the book	which he gave me.
They want a mechanic	who repairs computers.
This is the girl	whom her mother is calling.

Number of Sentences = 8 + 2 = 10

Exercise 4 - Simple Answers: Affirmative

Match the sentences and frame at least two sentences of your own following the patterns given below.

Are you going to work?	Yes, I am.
Can you drive a car?	Yes, I can.
Does Rita sleep well?	Yes, she does.
Did he say anything?	Yes, he did.
Is it a good film?	Yes, it is.
Sheela has already come.	So, she has.
He looks unwell.	Yes, he does.

Number of sentences = 7 + 7 + 2 + 2 = 18

Exercise 5 - Simple Answers: Negative

Match the sentences and frame at least two sentences of your own following the patterns given below.

Are you going to work?	No, I am not.
Can you drive a car?	No, I can't.
Does Rita sleep well?	No, she does not.
Did he say anything?	No, he didn't.
Is it a good film?	No, it is not.
Sheela has already come.	No, she has not.
He looks unwell.	No, he does not.

Number of sentences = 7 + 7 + 2 + 2 = 18

Exercise 6 - Simple Answers

Match the sentences and frame at least two sentences of your own following the patterns given below.

The apples are not good.	No, they are not.
She doesn't like fish.	No, she does not.
He can't help laughing.	No, he can't.
He is unwell.	No, he is not.
You are joking.	Oh no, I'm not.
Why did you beat him?	But I didn't.
You can't understand.	Yes, I can.
He won't come again.	But he will.
You don't know him.	Oh yes, I do.

Number of sentences = 9 + 9 + 2 + 2 = 22

Exercise 7 - Frame at least five sentences of your own following the patterns given below.

Stop talking.
Sit here.
Don't talk.
Be silent.
Please give me a glass of milk.
Open the window.
Shut the door.
May he live a hundred years!
May God save the earth.

Exercise 8 - Frame at least two sentences of your own following the patterns given below.

Hush! Don't disturb the class.
Alas! My friend has met with an accident.
Hurrah! They have won the match.
Bravo! We are going to Goa next week.
Ah! He is dead.
May he survive this crisis!
If only I were a scholar!
What a nice day!
How stupid of you to behave like this!
What a fool you are!
Oh! I'm having a terrible pain in stomach.

Miscellaneous Exercises

Exercise 9 - (Voice) Frame at least five sentences (Active + Passive) of your own following the patterns given below.

Active Voice	Passive Voice
Is Hari helping them?	Are they being helped by Hari?
What do you want?	What is wanted by you?
Have you helped him?	Has he been helped by you?
Who has done this?	By whom has it been done?
Where have you kept the bags?	Where have the bags been kept by you?
What did Ravi buy?	What was bought by Ravi?
Who taught you Math?	By whom were you taught Math?
What were you writing?	What was being written by you?
Had Hari finished the story?	Had the story been finished by Hari?
When will you return my money?	When will my money be returned by you?

QUIZ BOOKS

ENGLISH IMPROVEMENT

OTHERS LANGUAGE

ACTIVITIES BOOK

QUOTES/SAYINGS

BIOGRAPHIES/CHILDREN SCIENCE LIBRARY

Set Code: 02122 S

COMPUTER BOOKS

All books available at www.vspublishers.com

www.ingramcontent.com/pod-product-compliance
Lightning Source LLC
Chambersburg PA
CBHW080549230426
43663CB00015B/2761